Modern Boatworks

David S. Yetman

Bristol Fashion Publications, Inc.
Rockledge, Florida

Modern Boatworks -- *By David S. Yetman*

Published by Bristol Fashion Publications, Inc.

Copyright © 2001 by David S. Yetman. All rights reserved.

No part of this book may be reproduced or used in any form or by any means-graphic, electronic, mechanical, including photocopying, recording, taping or information storage and retrieval systems-without written permission of the publisher.

BRISTOL FASHION PUBLICATIONS AND THE AUTHOR HAVE MADE EVERY EFFORT TO INSURE THE ACCURACY OF THE INFORMATION PROVIDED IN THIS BOOK BUT ASSUMES NO LIABILITY WHATSOEVER FOR SAID INFORMATION OR THE CONSEQUENCES OF USING THE INFORMATION PROVIDED IN THIS BOOK.

ISBN: 1-892216-34-5
LCCN: 00-136118

Contribution acknowledgments

Inside Graphics: David S. Yetman.
Cover Design: David S. Yetman

Modern Boatworks -- By David S. Yetman

Modern Boatworks -- By David S. Yetman

Modern Boatworks -- By David S. Yetman

TABLE OF CONTENTS

Introduction   Page 9

Chapter One
Demystifying Diesel Fuel Injection   Page 11

Chapter Two
Demystifying Gasoline Fuel Injection   Page 23

Chapter Three
Two-Strokes for Tomorrow   Page 31

Chapter Four
Propulsion Choices   Page 39

Chapter Five
Bow Thrusters   Page 47

Chapter Six
Surface Drives   Page 51

Chapter Seven
Propeller Technology   Page 57

Chapter Eight
Trim Tabs: Control to the Max   Page 61

Chapter Nine
Surviving a Mechanical Emergency   Page 67

Modern Boatworks -- By David S. Yetman

Chapter Ten
Electronic Ignition Systems — Page 73

Chapter Eleven
Inverters: AC in A DC World — Page 77

Chapter Twelve
Shore-Power Systems — Page 85

Chapter Thirteen
Wiring Basics — Page 95

Chapter Fourte
Future Lights — Page 101

Chapter Fifteen
Antenna Basics — Page 105

Chapter Sixteen
Communications Afloat — Page 115

Chapter Seventeen
VHF at Home — Page 121

Chapter Eighteen
Surviving an Electrical Disaster — Page 129

Chapter Nineteen
CAD for Your Projects — Page 137

Chapter Twenty
Working On Fiberglass — Page 143

Chapter Twenty-One
Freshwater Systems — Page 157

Chapter Twenty-Two *Washdown Systems*	Page 165
Chapter Twenty-Three *Build a Folding Foot Rest*	Page 173
Chapter Twenty-Four *Customizing Your Instrument Panel*	Page 179
Chapter Twenty-Five *Non-Skid Pads*	Page 185
Chapter Twenty-Six *Get a Grip*	Page 189
Chapter Twenty-Seven *The Name Game*	Page 195
Chapter Twenty-Eight *Fender Addenda*	Page 199
Chapter Twenty-Nine *Propeller Resurrection*	Page 205
Chapter Thirty *Choosing the Correct Oil*	Page 213
Chapter Thirty-One *Oil and Analysis*	Page 219
Chapter Thirty-Two *Clean & Easy Oil Changes*	Page 225

Chapter Thirty-Three
Hanging by a Thread   Page 231

Chapter Thirty-Four
Drilling and Tapping   Page 243

Appendix A
Publication Credits   Page 247

Appendix B
Numbered and Lettered Sizes   Page 249

Appendix C
Decimal - Metric - Fractions Conversions   Page 251

About The Author   Page 259

Introduction

Boating for pleasure is a relatively recent phenomenon. For most of their history, boats were used for hunting, fishing, transportation, warfare and commerce. Besides, only the rich had any leisure time anyway.

Pleasure boating as we know it came into its own in the last half of the twentieth century with the growth of the middle class and the availability of lightweight engines and outboards to power mass-produced boats. The appearance of sophisticated navigational aids like Loran, GPS and radar at consumer-electronics prices has opened boating to even more people who would not have had the time or inclination to learn the rigors of navigating without them. At last count, nearly 13 million pleasure boats were registered in the United States alone.

Boating has benefited dramatically from advances in engine, electronic, navigational and materials technologies. With these advances has come a tidal wave of information about them, not always well disseminated and often not clearly explained. Many of the chapters of this book started out as magazine articles intended to explain some of the newer technologies and their benefits. Others are directed toward helping readers use the technologies or, in some cases, be prepared when they let them down.

Modern Boatworks covers a wide variety of topics, including mechanical, electrical, communication and maintenance information. It's not just another do-it-yourself text, although it includes some do-it-yourself projects. Its purpose is to stimulate, inform and assist boat owners who have an interest in technology and the hands-on aspect of operating, maintaining and improving their boats.

Even though not every reader will own a diesel engine, install a hatch, rework an electrical system or need to customize the instrument panel, they will still find valuable information here. The chapters are grouped by a tenuous commonality, but the book is meant to be browsed at the whim of the reader. Enjoy! And remember, the best things in life are afloat.

.

David S. Yetman

Chapter One
Demystifying Diesel Fuel Injection

Chances are that there will be an exciting, new, high-tech option available on your next new boat: a diesel engine.

Today's turbocharged, intercooled, electronically controlled fuel-injected diesel engines are as different from yesterday's smelly old clunkers as can be. Rudolph Diesel's compression-ignition engine, patented in 1892, was not a universal success despite the appeal of its apparent simplicity and reliability. The major stumbling block was a fuel system that relied on compressed air to blow the fuel/air mixture into the cylinders. It was a crude arrangement resulting in unreliable fuel-to-air ratios, limitations on speed and poor adjustment to the requirements of varying engine loads.

Diesels were restricted to use as stationary engines and power for large commercial vessels for nearly three decades before the advent of mechanically controlled, direct fuel injection. This allowed them to become the force they are today.

In its simplest state, the mechanically controlled fuel injection system, as shown in Figure 1, was comprised of a gear-driven high-pressure pump that delivered fuel through rigid metal tubing to an injector nozzle spraying fuel directly into the combustion chamber. Timing of the injection was pre-set by the pump's mechanical connection to the engine's crankshaft.

Later versions were improved by a mechanism that could advance the injection timing in response to increased engine speed, much like the centrifugal advance in an automotive ignition distributor.

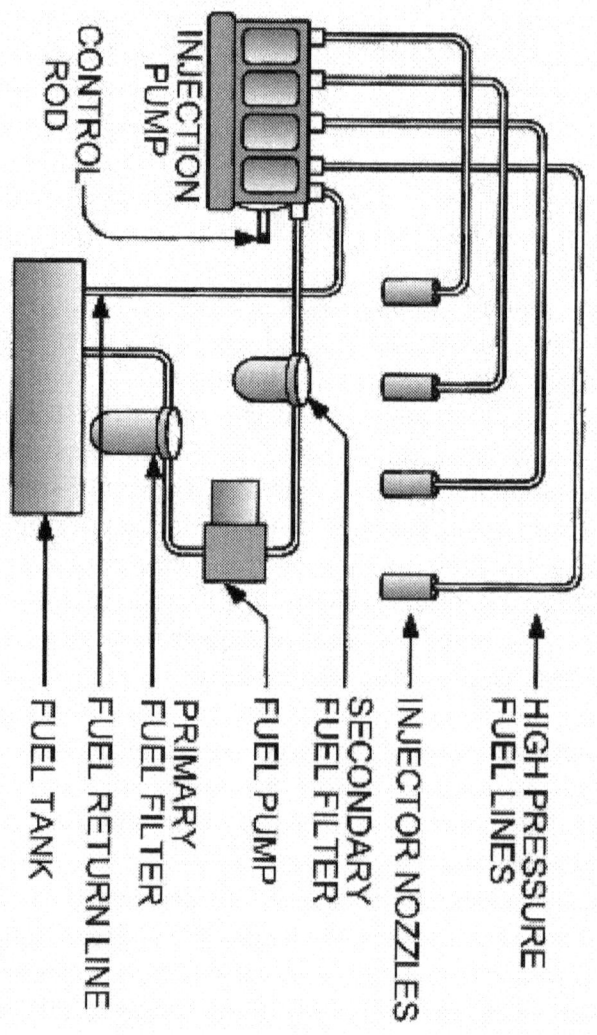

Figure 1-1
A mechanically controlled diesel fuel injection system.

The fuel-to-air ratio was determined by the volume of fuel per injection, which was metered at the pump and controlled by a mechanical linkage connected to the throttle. Each cylinder had a dedicated pump plunger, fuel delivery line and nozzle so that the pump for a six-cylinder engine looked like a miniature in-line engine itself.

The in-line injection pump at the heart of this ingenious system was a precisely engineered device whose complexity rivaled that of the engine it served, but the result was so effective that the system, with later advances in nozzle technology, is still in use on some modern engines. It is a tribute to their engineering that they meet current environmental standards, but the writing is on the wall: more restrictive future standards will be beyond their capabilities.

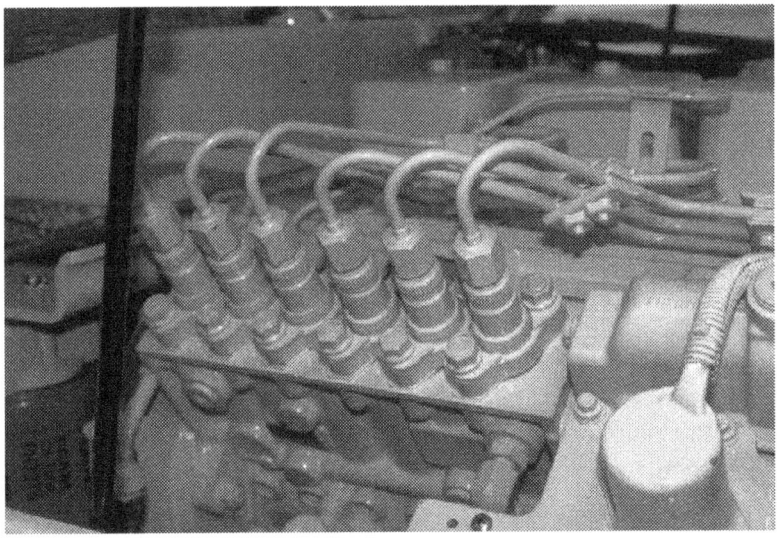

Figure 1-2
A mechanical fuel injection pump on a 6 cylinder Cummins.

Modern Boatworks -- By David S. Yetman

The demand for better performance and reduced emissions has accelerated the development of fuel injection technology. One result is the unit injector, which incorporates a high-pressure pump, injector valve and nozzle in a stand-alone unit for each cylinder. Because it eliminates the plumbing between the pump and the nozzle, it can operate at higher pressure, and its timing can be more precisely controlled, resulting in quieter operation, more power and better control over emissions. The pump plunger in most versions is mechanically actuated by a separate lobe on the engine's camshaft.

There are two basic types of unit injectors: mechanically controlled and electronically controlled. Mechanically controlled unit injectors typically use a complex rotating sleeve valve actuated by a rack or lever to vary the length of the injection pulse. The valve is normally open, allowing the fuel being pressurized by the pump plunger to bypass the nozzle and return to the fuel tank. When the timing dictates that injection is to begin, the bypass valve is closed, and the resulting pressure pulse is forced through the nozzle into the combustion chamber. The volume of the injection is determined by the length of time the bypass valve remains closed. Valve closing is determined by engine timing; opening time is determined by the position of the sleeve valve which is linked to the throttle.

The combination of extreme pressure created by the plunger (often greater than 15,000 psi) and the very small openings in the nozzle tip result in a finely atomized spray of fuel enhancing the efficiency of the combustion process.

The second category, electronically controlled unit injectors, mimics the operation of mechanical units except that the bypass valve is operated by a solenoid as shown in Figure 2. Control of injection timing and volume is completely independent of any engine state or function. Therein lies the key to the revolution in diesel engine technology.

Mechanically controlled systems, regardless of their sophistication, can respond to only two conditions, engine speed and throttle setting, because they are mechanically linked to the engine. Some early applications of electronic control merely replaced the mechanical linkage with a position sensor and an electric actuator attached to the control rod of the mechanical pump. This was a significant improvement because control could be based on conditions other than speed and throttle setting, but it still lacked the flexibility and precision that is afforded by direct electronic control.

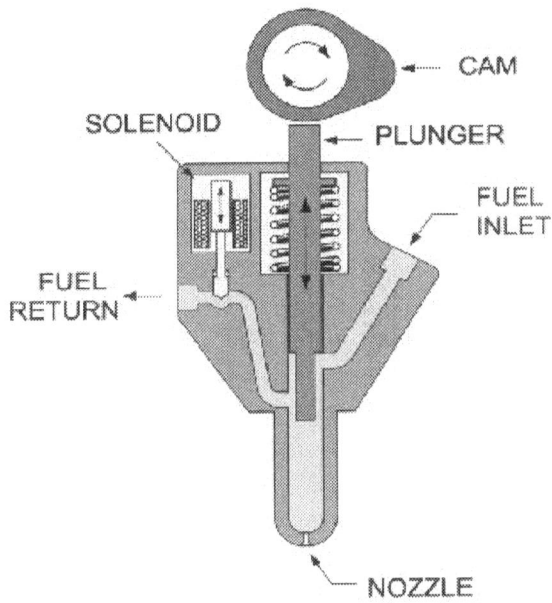

Figure 1-3
An electronically controlled fuel injector.

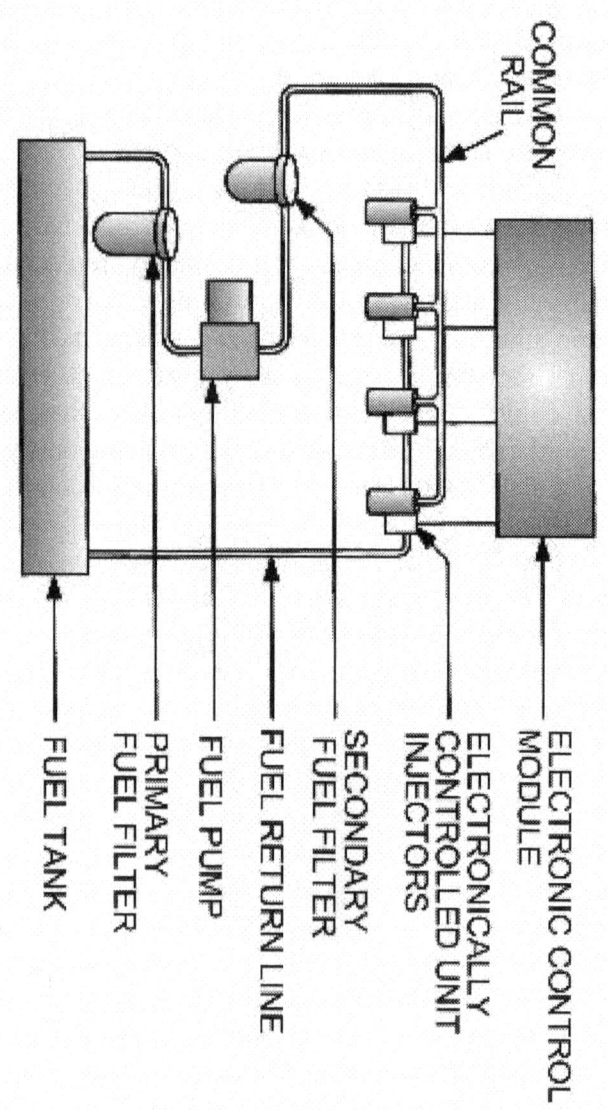

Figure 1-4

An electronically controlled diesel fuel injection system.

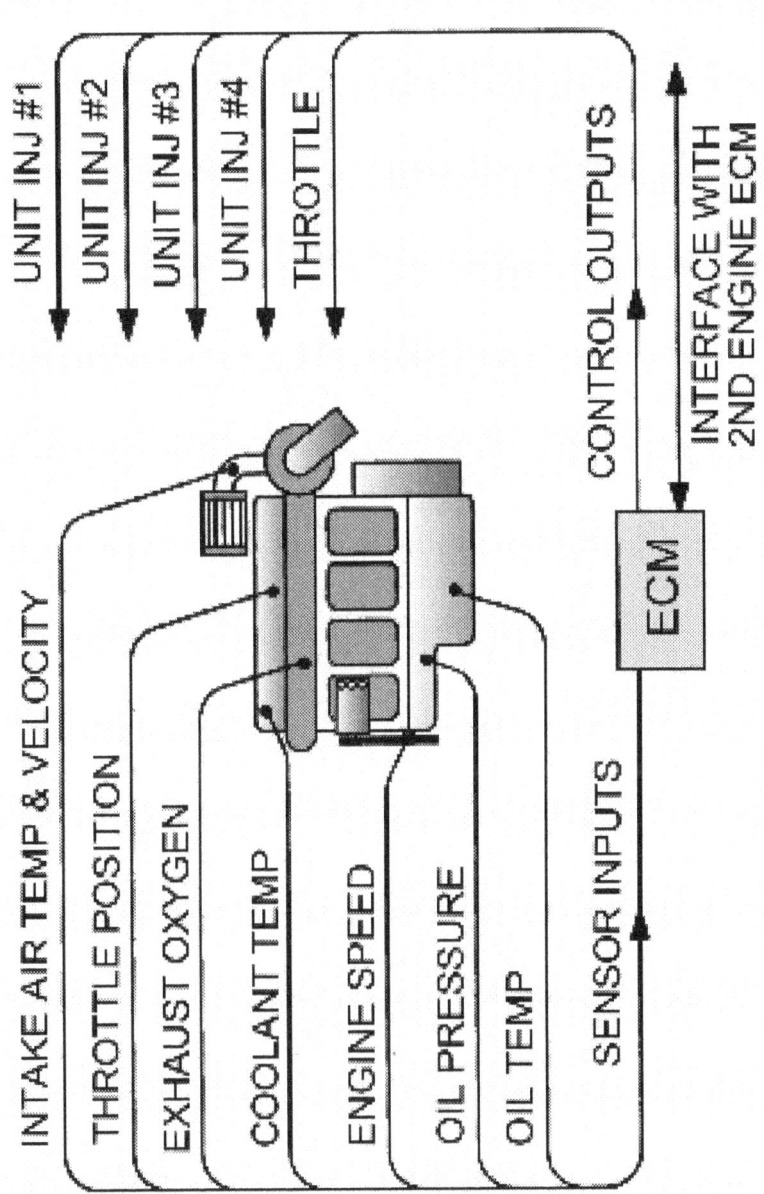

Figure 1-5
Logical diagram of an electronic fuel injection control system.

Modern Boatworks -- By David S. Yetman

The ability to electronically manage timing and volume of fuel delivery opens the door to very precise interactive microprocessor control of the injection system and, by extension, the combustion process itself. Such a system is shown in Figure 3.

Modern controllers, variously known as engine control units (ECU), electronic control modules (ECM) or electronic engine control modules (EECM) are thinly disguised computers that can monitor the input from sensors throughout the engine and its environment. The temperature of ambient air, engine oil and coolant, the oxygen content of exhaust gas, the velocity of intake air, the load on the engine, speed, throttle position and even the speed of a second engine are monitored by the control unit. It processes the information according to its internal program to create output signals that precisely tailor the operation of the fuel injection system to those conditions. Figure 4 is a logical diagram of the system control loop.

Most manufacturers of marine diesels still have a variety of fuel injection systems on their products, with in-line pumps and nozzles on older engines and electronic systems on newer or high-end products. Caterpillar is typical, using four different types of fuel injection for pleasure craft engines. Its 3208 series is still equipped with in-line pumps and nozzles; the 3116 and 3126 use mechanical unit injectors (MUI), while the 3176 and others use electronically controlled unit injectors (EUI). The latest innovation is the hydraulically operated, electronically controlled unit injector (HEUI). Instead of a camshaft to actuate the pump plunger, the HEUI uses hydraulic pressure from a branch of the engine's lubricating oil system. The intriguing part is that the hydraulic pressure in this sub-system could be varied by the ECM, giving Cat control over still another aspect of the process. HEUI was initially available only on

3412E marine engines, but it's slated to become the system of choice in the future.

The electronically controlled unit injector is usually credited with the diesel's current resurgence, but it just opened the door for the real star: the computer. Neither would have reached full potential in diesel technology without the other, but the combination means we will continue to see and benefit from advances in fuel injection and diesel performance. Diesel engines may never be exotic, but exciting high-tech will still apply.

What's Interactive?

Interactive is an overused but descriptive term describing a situation where two devices act upon each other. There are two levels of interaction: dumb and intelligent.

Dumb interaction takes place when two devices are rigidly linked so that one's action has a predictable and unavoidable consequence to the other. The two ends of a see-saw are interactive; one goes up as the other goes down. A speed governor is another example. When a vehicle reaches a pre-set speed, the governor senses it and reacts by limiting any further throttle opening or simply interrupts operation until the speed decreases.

On the other hand, if the governor could detect the difference between a side street and a highway and could change its limits to suit the circumstances, the interaction would be intelligent. Intelligent interaction takes place when input from a sensor is used by an intermediate device to make a decision affecting the output to the equipment being controlled. These days, the intermediate device is almost always a microprocessor, i.e., a computer.

Modern Boatworks -- By David S. Yetman

The perfect interactive device is a human being. For example, your eyes (the sensors) inform you (the input) that you are about to cross a substantial wake from another boat. Based on past experience (the program), your brain directs you (the output) to back off on the throttle and change course to cross the wake at an appropriate angle to insure your safety. When the sensors detect that the danger is past, the process is repeated and you go back to your original course and speed.

Electronically controlled fuel injection uses an identical process to manage all aspects of engine operation. A good example is the computer's management of the fuel-to-air ratio over a wide range of operating conditions. When its temperature sensors in the engine block and air-intake duct indicate that the engine and incoming air are both cold, the EEC's computer lengthens the time that each fuel injector valve stays open to increase the amount of fuel to ensure a rich mixture. As the engine warms up, the injection pulse is shortened and the fuel mixture is returned to normal. If the temperature of the incoming air rises because of an increase in outside temperature, the amount of fuel per injection is reduced further to compensate for the warmer, less dense air coming in.

The computer makes these decisions many times per second and adjusts its output based on its internal program and all of its inputs, not just those from the two temperature sensors mentioned. If the engine and air temperature are 165^0 and 78^0 and the engine speed is 1,800 rpm, its output could be different if the engine speed or other operating condition change even if the temperatures don't. The result is an engine that always operated in perfect response to its environment. That's interactive!

Modern Boatworks -- By David S. Yetman

Modern Boatworks -- By David S. Yetman

Chapter Two
Demystifying Gasoline Fuel Injection

Fuel injection has always had a magical ring to it, evoking visions of exotic systems that would effect dramatic improvements in the performance of internal combustion engines. The fuel-injected Chevrolet Corvettes of the early Sixties drew awe-struck crowds every time their hoods were opened to reveal a solid aluminum casting where the carburetor should have been. Never mind that irrigation pumps, electric generators, farm tractors and other mundane machinery had been powered by lumbering fuel-injected diesels for decades; fuel injection was exotic and hot.

Now 40 years later, fuel injection is ubiquitous in automobiles, where it's used in a number of versions, but the differences between types of fuel injection and their relative advantages are still not widely understood. The proliferation of descriptions hasn't helped the situation. Throttle-body, multi-port, common-rail and direct injection have been added to the old standbys (mechanical and electronic fuel injection) so that the torrent of technical terms threatens to inundate us. But now that the revolution is finally trickling down into marine use, it's time to take a closer look at the technology and its many advantages.

Fuel injection is a technology that replaces carburetion as a process to introduce fuel into an airflow to form a combustible mixture for an internal combustion engine. The carburetor relied on the venturi effect to coax the proper amount of fuel from a reservoir (float bowl) through a system of channels and out of an orifice (jet) into the airstream. The fact that later ones worked as well as they did is a tribute to 80 years of tinkering and refinement. A fuel injector is a relatively simple nozzle through which pressurized fuel is atomized and introduced into an airstream or directly into a combustion chamber. The method by which the injection is accomplished and controlled provided the first major change in the technology — the switch from mechanical to electronic control.

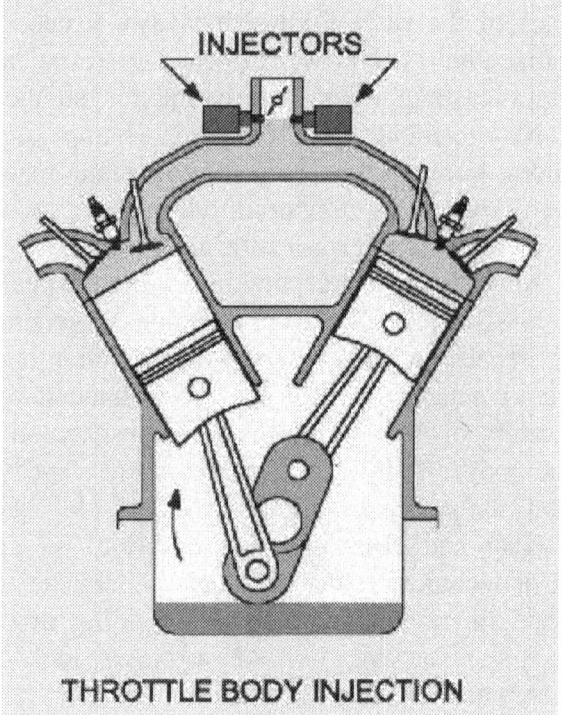

Figure 2-1

Mechanical fuel injection has been around since the 1920s but mainly used in diesel applications where fuel is injected directly into the combustion chamber. The pressure, timing and volumetric control of the injection is provided by a single gear-driven pump which has an individual cam-operated piston and fuel-delivery line to the injector for each cylinder of the engine. The only variables are the volume of each injection of fuel (controlled through a lever connected to the throttle linkage) and the timing, which adjusts the injection to match engine speed and power demand. The primary drawback was that the variability was mechanically tied to just two conditions, engine speed and throttle position. No compensation could be made for any other conditions that affect engine operation.

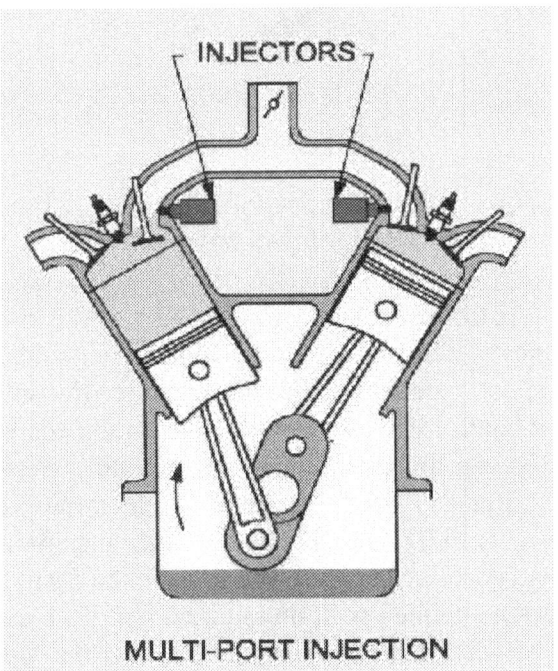

Figure 2-2

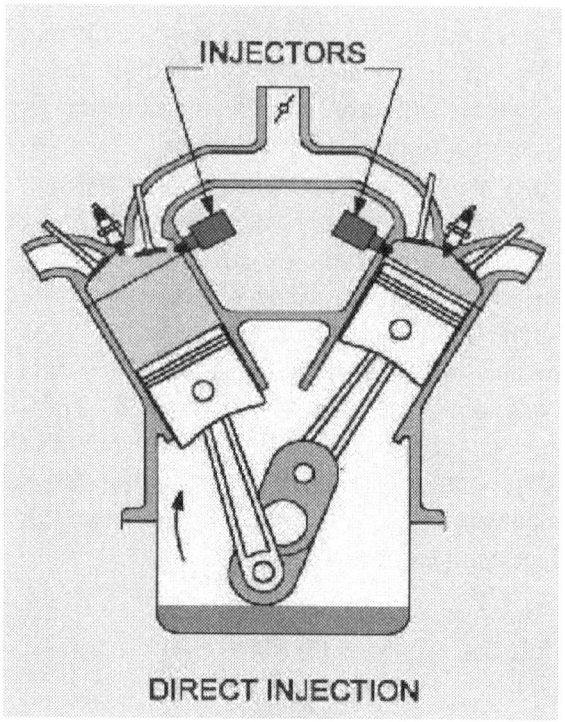
Figure 2-3

The three illustrations above show the various locations of for injector placement.

Electronic fuel injection or EFI (more properly, electronically controlled fuel injection) changed that. The invention of injectors with integral electric solenoid-operated control valves meant that the timing and volume of fuel being injected could be infinitely varied by electric signals from a remote electronic engine controller (EEC). The technology has benefited both diesel and gasoline engines. The injectors in gasoline EFI systems are supplied with pressurized fuel from a single, relatively inexpensive pump instead of the complex mechanical pump/controller of mechanical systems. The electronic controller makes adjustments in fuel delivery based on operational information from engine sensors, providing the flexibility that was missing in mechanically controlled units. Early analog controllers have been replaced with digital controllers (computers in disguise) whose operation also takes advantage of programs stored in their memory. The newest controllers can monitor many operating conditions including air, coolant and oil temperature, intake velocity, engine speed and load, throttle position and even listen for knocking. This information is combined with program instructions to determine and control the optimum fuel-delivery conditions as well as ignition timing. The result has been smoother and more powerful engines, increased fuel economy and greatly reduced emissions.

The original automotive application for EFI, and the one that trickled down first to marine use, is throttle-body fuel injection (TBI). One or more injectors are placed in the engine's intake manifold just below the throttle butterfly (as shown in Figure 1). The resulting fuel/air mixture is then shared by all the cylinders. In reality, TBI is the equivalent of electronically controlled carburetion but with the significant benefit of precise, interactive control of fuel and ignition conditions. It is also the least expensive form of EFI.

The next step up the performance ladder is multi-port fuel injection (MPI) where an injector is placed at the intake port of each cylinder just upstream of the intake valve (as shown in Figure 2). This placement allows the fuel to be introduced into a turbulent part of the airstream, providing better mixture of the fuel and air, which results in more efficient and complete combustion of the charge. The added cost of additional injectors and hardware is offset by better performance, fuel efficiency and the control of emissions.

Modern Boatworks -- By David S. Yetman

The latest form of fuel injection to be applied to gasoline engines is direct fuel injection (DFI) where the fuel is injected directly into the combustion chamber under very high pressure, imitating the system that diesels have used for decades (as shown in Figure 3). Several automotive manufacturers are developing DFI systems which they call common-rail systems. The common rail is a high-pressure manifold that delivers fuel to the injectors. The benefits of DFI promise still greater control over the combustion process and the resulting increase in fuel efficiency.

Curiously, because technology advances in the automotive world usually take several years to show up in marine use, the first widespread commercial application of DFI in gasoline engines is happening in outboard motors and being applied to two-stroke engines. Increasingly restrictive EPA emission guidelines have forced manufacturers of normally dirty two-stroke engines to look for ways to clean up their act. Many are making the switch to four-stroke technology as the easiest way out. Others, such as OMC, Mercury and Yamaha, have embraced DFI with mounting evidence of success. Their differing approaches are evidence of still another branching of fuel injection technology. OMC has licensed the FICHT system, which uses the injector solenoid valve's mechanical stroke to hammer the fuel charge through the injector nozzle. They claim the resulting increase in force does a better job of atomizing the fuel, enhancing the combustion process. Mercury's OptiMax technology, licensed from Orbital Engine Co., uses a more complex, low-pressure system to inject the fuel/air mixture directly into the combustion chamber.

Both systems take advantage of being able to hold off the introduction of fuel into the combustion chamber until the cylinder's exhaust port is closed by the rising piston, thus eliminating the introduction of unburned fuel into the exhaust system. The result is engines with all of the two-stroke's benefits (light weight, high power) and greatly reduced liabilities (smoke, pollution and rough idle). True, their cost is higher than equivalent traditional outboards, but there are relatively few instances where the application of technology has resulted in such a dramatic improvement between the old and the new.

It would be easy to credit the benefits of injected engines to the difference between carburetion and fuel injection. You could argue that electric solenoid-equipped injectors could have been run by a distributor-like device and result in some improvement, but that would ignore the real contributor to modern engine performance: the computer. Its interactive nature, the ability to read inputs from engine sensors, processes the information according to a program and then make changes in operating conditions as often as 50 times per second. This is the key difference.

The combination of performance benefits and government regulation will soon finalize the changeover from carburetors to fuel injection, so it won't be long before a set of highly polished Stromberg 97s or a squat Rochester 4-barrel shows up on the same museum shelf with a hand- crank phone and a telegraph key. We'll smile and remember, but we won't miss them.

Modern Boatworks -- By David S. Yetman

Chapter Three
Two-Strokes for Tomorrow

My neighbor at the marina has a four-year-old 200-horsepower outboard on his boat. It idles like a jackhammer, smokes like a landfill fire and usually needs to be re-started two or three times before it finally warms up. Once it does, it runs well, produces lots of useable power and uses an extraordinary amount of gas and oil. Another neighbor down the dock bought a new 200-horsepower outboard last year. It starts and stays running, produces almost no smoke and idles more like an automobile than an outboard motor. He's a very happy in spite of the motor's five-figure price tag because he's enjoying outstanding performance, increased fuel economy and significantly reduced oil consumption.

The difference between the two is the difference between traditional two-stroke technology and the new electronically controlled, fuel-injected breed of two-strokes.

The changes brought about this startling improvement are simple in concept but quite complex in implementation. The best way to fully appreciate them is to start with a good understanding of the basic two-stroke.

The two-stroke engine (technically a two-stroke-cycle engine) was invented late in the 19th century but wasn't a commercial success until just after 1900, when the first patents were issued. Its popularity has persisted because of its light weight, general reliability and, above all, its simplicity. A four cylinder version could have as few as nine major moving parts. It came into its own after WW II as the power plant of choice for motorbikes, cars and even small trucks in countries where economical transportation was needed to support recovering economies. Its later development was accelerated by the worldwide growth of the motorcycle and pleasure boat markets.

It gets its name from the fact that its power cycle is completed in just two strokes of the piston, one down and one up, on a single rotation of the crankshaft. The entire sequence is shown in Figure 1, which depicts the single-cylinder two-stroke engine in its simplest form. All of the intake, exhaust, and fuel transfers are accomplished through ports in the cylinder walls, where the piston acts as a valve, exposing or closing off the ports as it slides by. Although only three ports are shown for simplicity's sake, in reality some high-performance engines may have five to seven of them, with the most emphasis placed on multiple transfer ports for increased efficiency.

The cycle begins in view "A" of Figure 1 where the fuel/air charge has been compressed at the top of the cylinder and is ignited by the spark plug, exerting downward pressure on the piston. As the piston travels downward in view "B" it exposes the exhaust port, allowing the exhaust gases to escape and begins to close off the carburetor's intake port. As it does so, it compresses the fuel/air charge which has been drawn into the crankcase. In view "C," the piston has reached the bottom of its travel, opening the transfer port to allow the compressed fuel/air charge to escape from the crankcase into the cylinder above. In view "D," the piston closes the transfer and exhaust ports as it compresses the fuel/air mixture into the top of the cylinder. Further piston movement opens the intake port, allowing more fuel and air to rush into the void in the crankcase created by the upward travel of the piston. When the piston has fully compressed the fuel/air charge at the top of its travel, ignition will occur to begin the cycle again.

Like any technology that has been around for a century, this one has seen many variations and incremental improvements. The primitive piston-actuated intake port in the cylinder wall has been replaced in some versions with a port directly into the crankcase that is controlled by a reed valve or a rotating disc valve on the crankshaft, both of which offer more flexibility and better control of operating conditions. These improvements, along with the ability to design highly tuned intake and exhaust systems, helped two-strokes keep pace with growing expectations but did little to address the efficiency and environmental baggage that they carried.

One of the primary contributors to the early two-strokes' simplicity was the absence of a recirculating lubrication system. Since the intake stream eventually reached all the parts that need to be lubricated, oil was simply mixed with the fuel and then burned in the combustion process, contributing to the cloud of exhaust smoke that became the two-stroke's trademark. The amount of oil used was governed by the mix ratio, not by engine needs. Modern two-strokes are equipped with oiling systems fed from a separate reservoir. They precisely meter the oil to match changing operating conditions, greatly reducing excess oil burning. But since oil is still burned during operation, this has only reduced, not eliminated, the smoke.

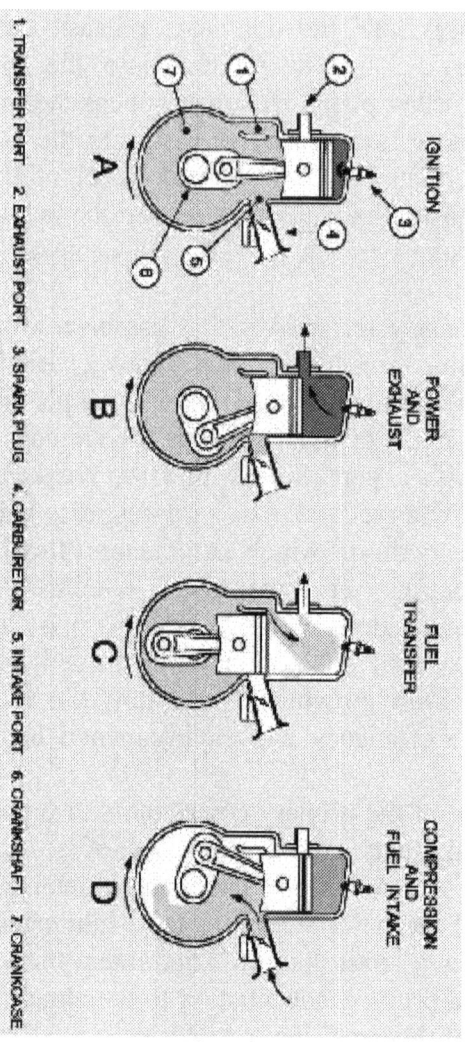

Figure 3-1

Operation of the basic two-stroke engine.

Smoke and pollution problems are also compounded by unburned fuel and oil in the exhaust, the result of having the transfer and exhaust ports open simultaneously (Figure 1C), allowing some of the incoming fuel mixture to enter the exhaust system. Careful exhaust-system tuning eased the impact of this condition but couldn't eliminate its contribution to both inefficiency and pollution. The real solution had to wait for the introduction of direct fuel injection (DFI) and electronic engine control (EEC).

Direct fuel injection has been used in diesel engines for decades. In its basic form it consists of an injector inserted into the combustion chamber through which fuel is sprayed under high pressure. It also has been applied to some high-performance gasoline-powered German cars but has not been introduced more widely because its mechanical pump and control systems were inflexible and expensive. The more recent introduction of solenoid-controlled injector valves has opened up new applications because injector operation is no longer controlled by a remote mechanical pump but by electronic commands applied directly to the injector. These commands are supplied by the EEC.

Electronic engine control is computer control by another name. EEC systems have been used in automotive applications since the Eighties but have become significantly more refined in the past few years. In many applications they monitor every condition that may affect engine operation, including engine and air temperature, intake velocity, throttle opening, engine load, exhaust gases and even listen for engine knocking. Based on these inputs and the program in its memory, the computer makes decisions about ignition and injection timing, then sends the appropriate signals to the ignition system and fuel injectors.

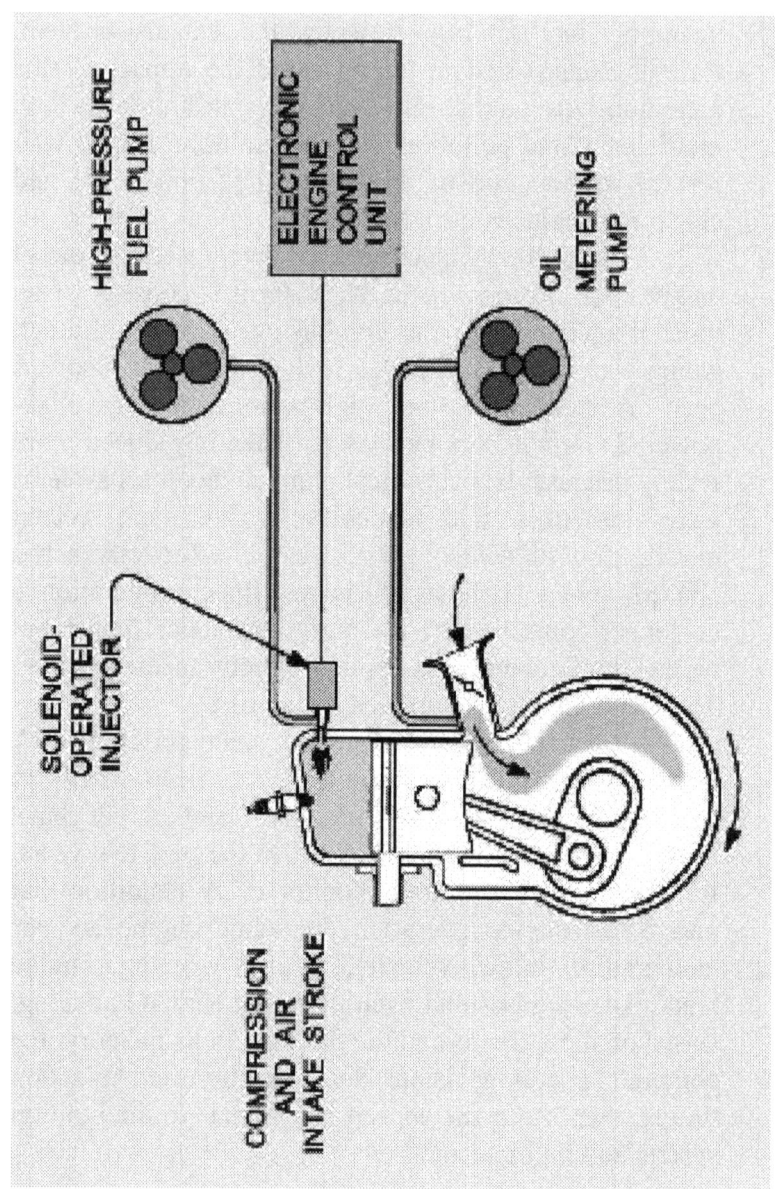

Figure 3-2

Direct fuel injection (DFI) two-stroke engine.

The combination of DFI and EEC has been a crucial factor in the dramatic improvements in two-stroke engines. The primary improvement has been the elimination of fuel from the intake stream. Only air and oil now enter the crankcase (Figure 2), so when the exhaust and transfer ports are open simultaneously, no unburned fuel escapes. The fuel isn't injected into the cylinder until just before ignition, and when it is, it comes in the form of a very fine mist and in amounts precisely tailored to the exact operating conditions at the time. The result is less smoke, more complete combustion, greater fuel economy and smoother operation.

At least for now, the down-side is cost and complexity. There are competing technologies, OMC's FICHT and Mercury's OptiMax (the latter the more complex of the two), but both are likely to require more expert maintenance than traditional two-strokes. Other manufacturers are using various levels of electronic controls, but the long-term prospect for those that do not switch to DFI is probably bleak. The combination of EPA regulations and the performance expectations of consumers will probably mean the demise of traditional two-strokes. This will leave DFI engines and their variations to carry on as the two-strokes for tomorrow.

Modern Boatworks -- *By David S. Yetman*

Chapter Four
Propulsion Choices

One of the defining aspects of a boat is its propulsion system. It's what makes powerboats work. There was a time when deciding how to power a boat was much simpler. You could choose a paddlewheel or a new-fangled screw propeller, either of them powered by a steam engine.

Modern boaters have a much wider choice of power, although practically all are some form of internal-combustion engine. Regardless of where or how it's mounted, it will almost certainly drive a propeller.

At first glance, that would appear to be fairly restrictive, but in reality there's a wide array of propulsion-system configurations to choose from. Each has its strong points and drawbacks. Some are highly specialized. Others are rarely seen or just coming into their own, but chances are good that you'll be faced with a choice between some of them when you consider your next boat purchase.

Here's a look at the pros and cons of the options, the first six of which are variations based on an inboard engine.

The traditional inboard configuration is a forward-mounted engine/gearbox combination directly coupled to a propeller shaft that exits through the bottom of the hull.

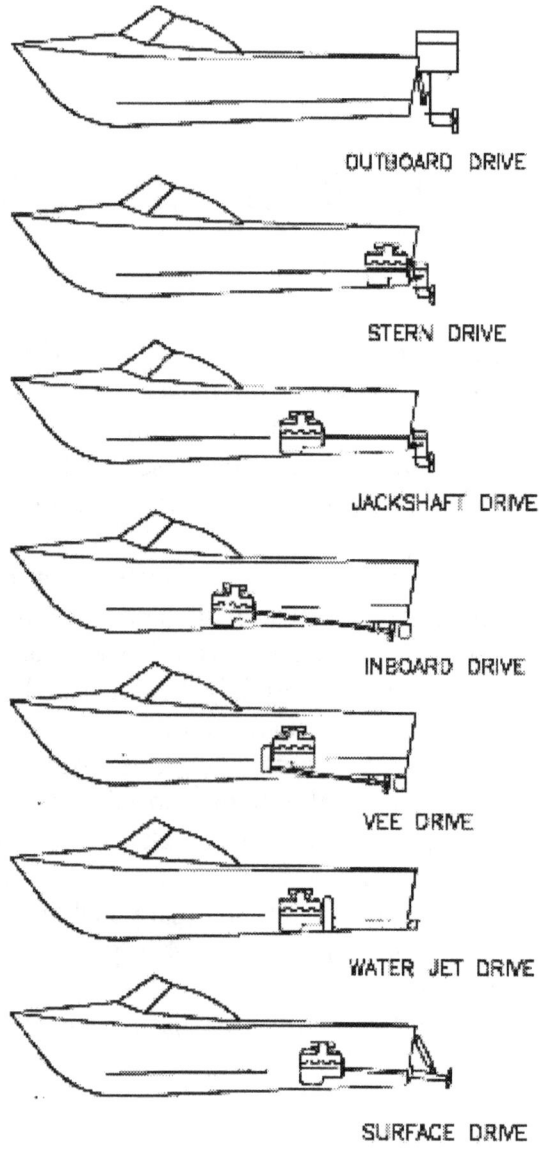

Figure 4-1

The layout of various propulsion systems.

Pros: simplicity. There are fewer power-robbing gears and joints to maintain. Engine exhaust and cooling systems are less complicated than inboard/outboard arrangements. The boat's center of gravity is farther forward, which can enhance handling. The aft cockpit and transom areas remain unobstructed and uncluttered.

Cons: the engine occupies forward space and may intrude on cabin accommodation. In single-screw installations, the boat's maneuverability will suffer in comparison to an outdrive or outboard configuration (especially in reverse), where prop-walk can be a problem.

In a V-drive configuration, the engine and gearbox are turned around so that the gearbox is forward. The gearbox is designed so that its aft-facing output is low enough to mate with a prop shaft that runs aft under the engine. The arrangement is not common on small boats but is often seen on Down East express cruisers.

Pros: The engine can be mounted farther aft where it doesn't impinge on cabin or helm accommodations. Gearbox control cable or linkage routes are more direct.

Cons: the engine must be mounted higher to clear the prop shaft underneath, raising the boat's center of gravity and often requiring an engine box in the cockpit area. Prop-shaft rotation is opposite the engine's.

A jackshaft drive is a hybrid system that uses a long drive shaft to connect a forward-mounted inboard engine to an outdrive unit mounted in the transom.

Pros: Weight distribution and center of gravity benefit from the low forward-engine mounting position. Universal or constant-velocity joints in the drive shaft can eliminate critical alignment requirements. It incorporates the trim and maneuverability benefits of an outdrive and adds the option of using dual counter-rotating propellers with an inboard engine.

Cons: Slightly more expensive than a comparable stern-drive system. The added complexity of the outdrive can result in higher maintenance costs than a traditional inboard arrangement.

The stern-drive or inboard/outboard system has a transom-mounted outdrive directly coupled to the engine mounted just forward of the transom. It's far and away the most widely used system employing an inboard engine and most appropriate for the boats that make up the heart of the pleasure boat market (14 to 30 feet). This helps to explain its popularity.

Pros: It's a compact propulsion system that concentrates most of the mechanical components in one area at the stern. It includes the trim and maneuverability benefits of an outdrive and delivers power efficiently because the prop angle can be trimmed to suit the attitude of the boat.

Cons: The complexity of the system can result in higher maintenance costs than a traditional inboard arrangement. Servicing can be difficult because of the system's position low and aft in the boat. Weight distribution, especially in smaller boats, is heavily biased aft.

Water-jet propulsion systems combine an inboard engine connected to a pump that takes in raw water and forcefully expels it through an orifice to propel the boat. They're not new, but seem to have gained popularity for pleasure boats lately, at least partly because they're ubiquitous in the personal watercraft industry. They've also gained credibility because of their use by premium boatbuilders such as Hinckley and Little Harbor.

Pros: The elimination of the propeller, prop shaft and rudder reduces the boat's draft and cuts down on noise and vibration.

Cons: The addition of the pump, plus a complex directional orifice and reversing mechanism, add considerable cost to the boat. In many cases, there's no disconnect between the engine and the pump, so the boat is under way unless the engine is stopped.

Surface drives are available in many different forms, from complex systems like Arneson drives to outboard motors with shortened shafts to lift the prop partially out of the water. All share a common goal of enabling the use of surface-piercing propellers to increase speed and efficiency. (See Chapter 6 for an in-depth look at their operation.)

Pros: Top-of-the-line surface drives provide increases in speed and fuel efficiency of 15 to 30 percent.

Cons: Surface drives can add 10 percent or more to the cost of a boat. Hull design and weight must be carefully matched to the drives to realize their full benefit. Drive types that extend well aft of the transom can require additional maintenance and present a considerable safety hazard to persons in the water.

Outboard motors drive more pleasure boats than any other propulsion system because of their favorable power-to-weight ratio, portability, and wide range of sizes. That's not going to change in the foreseeable future, but outboards are undergoing sweeping changes in order to comply with increasingly stringent environmental rules.

Pros: Outboards are compact, concentrating most mechanical components in one easily serviced module. They deliver power more efficiently than most inboard systems because their prop angle can be trimmed to suit the boat's attitude. Their position aft of the transom results in more room in the cockpit and greater maneuverability. Their installation cost is low, and they're available in a wide range of sizes, especially in the lower power range that small boats require.

Cons: They present more obstructions and clutter at the transom, which can be a problem for fishermen. Two stroke versions are generally noisier than inboards. Their fuel efficiency suffers in comparison to inboards of similar power. They burn their lubricants, exhaust more smoke and cause more pollution.

No discussion of propulsion choices for boats between 14 and 30 or so feet could be complete without acknowledging the gulf that separates the inboard from the outboard. Such a discussion is dangerous, not unlike religious or political preferences. Adherents on both sides will never change their preference, no matter what, but the changing outboard landscape will directly affect propulsion choices in the future. Thus, at least a review is in order.

The cost of many inboards traditionally has benefited from their origins as automobile or truck engines. Economies of scale, where engines have been produced by the millions, have been passed on to boaters in the form of lower costs. Outboards, designed and produced for boats alone, have not had the same advantage but instead reaped the benefits of being two-stroke engines. These have significantly fewer parts and are therefore less expensive to build. The result is that cost-per-horsepower has been remarkably similar in the horsepower range where outboard and stern-drive units compete when the added cost of installing a stern-drive is factored in. With the impending demise of the traditional two-stroke engine, the balance is changing. (See Chapter 3 for a closer look at the revolution in two-strokes.)

In the scramble to meet increasingly stringent EPA guidelines, outboard makers are taking two paths; switching to four-stroke engines or embracing advanced two-stroke technology such as direct pressurized fuel injection and other complex schemes to reduce the inherent emissions of two-strokes. Neither approach is inexpensive.

POWER	AVERAGE PRICE	COST/HP
Traditional two-stroke outboard	$8,124.00	$71.00
Injected two-stroke outboard	$8,939.00	$74.00
Four-stroke outboard	$9,919.00	$86.00
Stern drive (135HP)	$6,114.00	$45.00

Figure 4-2
The cost.

The easiest way to grasp comparative costs is to look at a power level where four options (sterndrive, traditional two-stroke outboard, fuel-injected two-stroke outboard and four-stroke outboard) currently compete) at 100 to 135 horsepower. This unscientific survey of manufacturers' suggested list prices at the time of writing was based at this power level because it provided a look at the widest number of choices, it allowed the inclusion of stern drives and all the units in the survey had four-cylinder engines.

At this power level, the stern drive enjoys a $29-per-horsepower advantage over the injected two-stroke outboard. If you compare the two at 225hp instead of 115hp, the difference narrows but is still a sizable $20 advantage for the stern drive.

As long as there are small boats, there will be outboards. But as they are forced to become increasingly complex, the cost of ownership and maintenance will continue to demand a premium over automotive-based inboards in the power range where the two compete. To this the legions of diehard outboard enthusiasts will collectively reply, "Yeah? So what?"

Chapter Five
Bow Thrusters

BOW thrusters are a form of propulsion, too, but they propel things sideways. If you've ever watched in amazement as a large ferry boat eased away from a tight berth, did a 180_ pirouette in its own length and unceremoniously headed off, chances are you already know what a bow or stern thruster can do. Many large vessels such as cruise ships employ multiple thrusters to provide extraordinary mobility, a necessity in remote ports where tugboats are unheard of.

My initial doubts about the usefulness of a bow thruster in the environment where I keep my boat were dispelled the first time I needed one to get under way with a 15-knot breeze pressing the boat directly against the dock. Pushing the joystick on the control panel to the right caused the bow to swing 30 degrees to starboard in about five seconds, allowing me to put the transmission in gear and depart cleanly. It was a convincing display of the thruster's performance under adverse conditions. The same maneuver without it would have required some adept use of springlines and considerably more time.

The transition from outboard- or stern-drive jockey to novice single-screw skipper can be much less traumatic with the aid of a thruster. A misjudged turn in tight quarters can be corrected without a fuss by a quick push of the joystick. You can perform a 180-degree turn without putting the transmission in gear and leave a dock cleanly without assistance from shore personnel.

It does require some vigilance, though. After my first stop at the fuel dock, the dockhand was about to lean into the bow rail to push me off when I switched on the bow thruster and the rail moved rapidly away from his grip. Thankfully, he was able to catch himself in time to avoid an unplanned swim.

Discussions of a bow thruster often center on the potential savings of having one in place of a second engine, especially if the boat is diesel-powered. Were the choice that simple, the savings would be unchallenged: $3,500 and up for the thruster vs. $20,000 and up for a second engine.

Figure 5-1

Bow thruster location below the waterline.

Of course, it's more complex than that. A single large engine and propulsion system may cost almost as much as two small ones. Maintenance of a single will be less than twins but not by half. Proponents of twins will also point out the reliability of having a way to get home if one engine dies. They'll also bring up the subject of maneuverability.

Although a bow thruster provides better mechanical advantage for swinging the bow around, twin screws have a decided advantage in some situations, like backing into a berth or backing down on a fish. This isn't to say the thruster provides no benefit in reverse. One trick I'm still learning and refining is to back into a berth by turning the rudder far enough to port to neutralize the boat's tendency to prop-walk to starboard (essentially allowing the boat to back down straight). This allows me to steer with the bow thruster. The maneuver requires practice and good hand-eye coordination, but it can be very effective when doing something normally not much fun in a single-screw vessel.

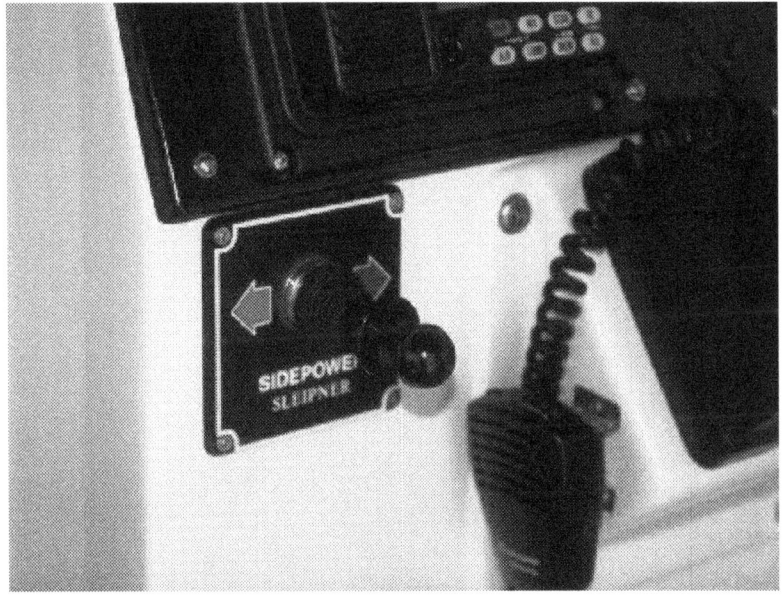

Figure 5-2

The bow thruster controller at the helm.

No cut-and-dried answer exists to the thruster-vs.-twins argument. There are too many variables, preferences and prejudices. Perhaps a more worthwhile comparison is between a single-screw boat. With or without a bow thruster, the thruster wins hands-down. After using one for two seasons, I'd spend the money again in a heartbeat.

If you're not a very experienced boater yet considering a medium-size or larger single-screw inboard vessel, by all means opt for a bow thruster. Even if you're good enough that you rarely use it, it will add considerably to the resale value of the boat. It may even occasionally prevent you from providing gratuitous dockside entertainment.

Chapter Six
Surface Drives

Performance is pervasive in discussions about powerboats, but it has many definitions. For many owners and builders, performance is narrowly defined in terms of speed and acceleration. When looking for ways to enhance performance, they're tempted to rely on the old hot-rodders' adage: "There's no substitute for cubic inches." Adding power is a relatively simple solution, especially at the design stage, and in cases where a large increase is needed, it may be the best one.

But there are broader aspects of performance that brute force will not enhance, and in some cases may even be detrimental.

Performance can also be measured in terms of efficiency, economy, maneuverability and the ability to go places where other boats can not. Efficiency is a particularly intriguing part of that list because it implies you can get something for nothing. The cost of Twin Disc/Arneson surface drives is a long way from nothing, but they provide many of the benefits on the list and then some. Mention Arneson to most people and they immediately think of ultra-high-performance racing boats, but the benefits can be enjoyed by everyday cruisers, too.

Though several surface drives are on the market, Howard Arneson's design offers a unique set of features. A majority of its machinery resides completely above the water line and outboard of the hull. Only a small skeg and the lower half of the propeller are in the water while under way. It eliminates the need for a rudder because the entire drive unit pivots horizontally (like a standard outdrive) to provide directional thrust. In addition, the depth of the propeller can be adjusted from the helm in response to varying load and sea conditions. The effect is like being able to vary the pitch of your prop while under way. Finally, it takes full advantage of the efficiency of surface-piercing propellers.

Arneson drives consist of an articulated propeller shaft encased in a long, tapered thrust tube that pivots on a joint within a flexible bellows at the transom. Models for boats from 30 to 200 feet position the propeller from three to 10 feet behind the transom. Each drive is equipped with two hydraulic cylinders. The vertical cylinder allows 15 degrees of trim to control propeller depth (Figure 1), and the steering cylinder provides 40 degrees of horizontal motion (Figure 2). The combination of the two with the thrust tube provides a perfectly triangulated positioning structure to locate the propeller.

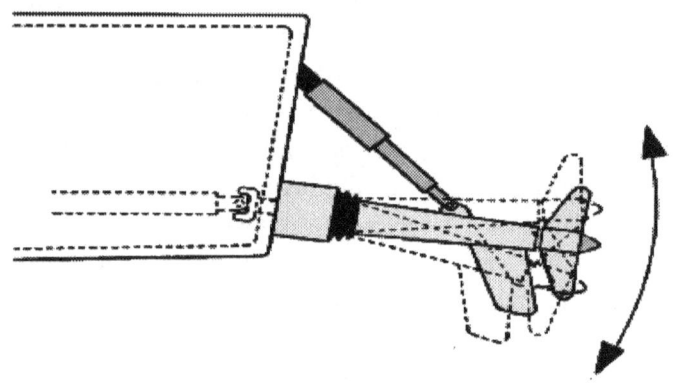

Figure 6-1
Side view of a surface drive showing vertical position options.

The increased efficiency provided by the Arneson drive has two sources. The first is the lack of any drag-inducing structure in the water. Even the slickest outdrive, the fairest keel or the smoothest rudder creates drag and turbulence in the water. Drag consumes power, and the turbulence interferes with the operation of the propeller, a double-whammy. The second source is a surface-piercing propeller.

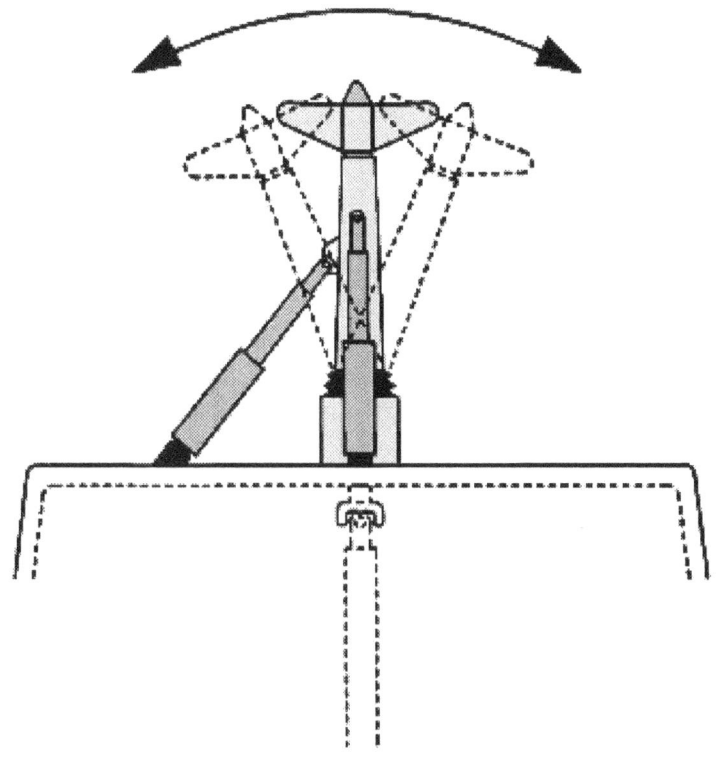

Figure 6-2

Top view of a surface drive showing steering action.

Modern Boatworks -- By David S. Yetman

For most people, a propeller that operates efficiently with its top half out of the water is a contradiction in terms. Intuitively we assume that the friction of each blade piercing the surface of the water twice in each revolution and the loss of motive power when the blade is out of the water would result in a loss of performance. In reality, power is conserved by keeping half of the propeller free of friction and turbulence, allowing more to be applied to the half below the waterline. When that's combined with the absence of drag from other machinery in the water and the propeller's optimum operating position in the flat water flowing undisturbed from under the hull, the result is increased efficiency. More of the engine's power is delivered where it matters — the water.

There are other benefits too. The location, well aft of the transom, eliminates restrictions on propeller size, allowing the designer to specify whatever is most suitable for the task. Moving the propellers aft also eliminates the noise, vibration and pounding they would normally transmit directly up to the hull, resulting in a smoother, quieter ride. The absence of restrictions resulting from propeller-shaft angle requirements also frees the designer to locate engines in the most advantageous position, even just ahead of the transom, moving the source of more noise and vibration away from populated areas of the boat. This gives them much greater leverage in steering the boat, resulting in better maneuverability and tighter turns. The effect is the same as mounting outboard motors on an extension bracket.

Finally, with far less machinery protruding below the hull, you can venture into shallow areas you could only previously enjoy through binoculars.

With such a list of impressive benefits, why are surface drives not offered on more boats? Three reasons:

Cost. The benefits are not free. Italian builder Antago offers a stylish 21-meter (70 ft) cruiser with the buyer's choice of conventional or Arneson drives. The Arneson option adds about 10 percent to the cost. Twin Disc's suggested list price for a single drive begins at about $7,000 for the smallest ASD-6 model to $130,000 for the largest. While these prices include an extensive package of peripheral components such as control cylinders, lubrication systems and maintenance aids, they do not include the cost of installation.

Safety: Propellers churning several feet abaft the transom can present an overt danger to persons in the water, especially one overboard. Many pleasure-craft builders reduce the danger by adding an extended swim platform, often with side curtains, to protect people from the propellers and drives from collisions during docking maneuvers.

Backing down: Surface drives have a reputation for being poor performers in reverse, but much of the reputation is a hold-over from the days when they were used almost exclusively with cleaver-type propellers on racing boats. According to Twin Disc, modern "round-ear" high-performance propellers have evolved to the point where they offer nearly all the top-end performance benefits of cleavers while retaining good performance in reverse. They cite the example of a large fleet of Arneson-equipped commercial fishing boats that operate quite efficiently while dragging their nets in reverse.

Arneson literature emphasizes the importance of a close working relationship between drive engineers and the boat's designer to obtain optimum results. The most important aspect of their collaboration is to insure proper hull shape. Notched hulls generally are not encouraged because of their reduced area in contact with the water. Hulls must have sufficient wetted surface to facilitate easy planing, since the advantage of the Arneson drive is primarily realized when on plane. The hull must be free of hook or rocker; the placement of water intakes, outlets, transducers and other interruptions must be sufficiently forward of the drives to avoid any disturbance of the clean, smooth flow of water from under the transom.

Highly developed equipment often becomes highly specialized as it evolves, yet the result can be greatly increased performance that is only useful in narrow applications. A hydroplane, for example, is eminently well suited to winning races, but it's nearly useless as a weekend cruiser. Surface drives aren't quite that specialized, but their performance benefits are attained through features that can make them unsuitable for some applications and too costly for others. Their use on dive or rescue boats, for example, is inappropriate because of the increased danger to anyone in the water. For that reason (and the need to operate in very shallow or obstruction- filled water), many military craft that would normally benefit from the Arneson drive are equipped with jet drives instead.

From a cost standpoint, situations exist where an upgrade in engine power will provide more performance-per-dollar than surface drives, especially on smaller, less expensive boats. Those restrictions aside, they can provide remarkable advantages when properly integrated into a boat whose intended use has been carefully considered during the design process. The manufacturer claims that the difference in performance between conventional drives and Arneson drives is a 15 to 30 percent increase in both speed and fuel efficiency. That's more than just scratching the surface.

Chapter Seven
Propeller Technology

The basic idea behind marine propellers is surprisingly old. The Greeks and the Egyptians before them used screw-like devices to move water for irrigation and to bail leaking ships nearly 3,000 years ago. But we usually attribute the invention of modern props to Francis Petit Smith and John Ericsson, who patented several types in 1836. Several people before them had attempted to propel watercraft with various screw-based devices, but none were successful enough to catch on and endure. Between 1836 and 1890, Smith and Ericsson's designs went through several stages of improvement before settling into a form we'd recognize as a modern propeller. Unless you look closely, you'd think that propellers have changed very little in the ensuing hundred or so years, but of course they have.

The change in propeller design over that time has been gradual and driven by the requirements of more powerful engines and new drives. Improvements were made possible by better materials, greater understanding of hydrodynamics and more efficient manufacturing methods. Some of the most striking changes have taken place in props designed for outboard and I/O applications where very aggressive pitch angles have become commonplace. Other important differences are more in the way props are used than how they're designed. Dual counter-rotating outdrives are a prime example. Their

Modern Boatworks -- By David S. Yetman

added cost and complexity are overshadowed by the significant increase in efficiency and performance they provide, but the props are not very different from most others.

Boatbuilders and designers continue to expand the use of exotic composite materials, but mainstream propeller manufacturers seem to stick with tried and true materials — aluminum, bronze, nibral, and stainless steel. For larger outboards and outdrives, aluminum is the low-cost leader, while stainless is the choice for higher performance and durability. For inboards and larger props, the choices are bronze and nibral (an alloy of nickel, bronze and aluminum). Several manufacturers offer non-metallic props, but they usually advertise their products for low- to medium-power engines on smaller boats and tout their ability to protect drive components from shock or their suitability as lightweight, inexpensive spares.

Propeller makers' apparent conservatism doesn't extend to manufacturing, though. Most take full advantage of computer-aided design and computer-aided-manufacturing to keep up with manufacturing technology and remain competitive. The result is propellers that run smoother and perform better. Computers are also an important tool at the other end of the supply chain, where their increasing use for evaluating, truing and balancing at local propeller shops directly benefits the user.

Recreational boaters have reaped benefits from continuing evolution in the form of a greatly expanded array of propellers that allow them to tailor their power train precisely to the way their boats are used. If there's a detectable trend in boating today, it's the quest for performance, and it shows up in the growing number of four-blade props and the increasing sales of stainless steel props. Boaters are willing to pay the additional cost of stainless props and accept the possibility of greater drive train damage in the event of accidental contact with an obstruction in exchange for an edge in performance. Everyone seems to be looking for those last few knots.

Stainless steel, however, is not a magic metal. Simply taking the design for an aluminum propeller and manufacturing it in stainless add cost, strength, and weight, but do almost nothing for performance. The advantage that stainless steel offers is its density and strength, which permit a propeller to be designed with thinner cross sections and more aggressive contours without losing rigidity or durability. It's the more radical design that adds to performance, not the material itself. Thus, unless the propeller is specifically designed to take advantage of the metal's qualities, the extra cost and weight are wasted.

Most of the work that goes into choosing the right propeller will have been done at the factory, where the boat's hull design, length, weight, power and intended use will have been carefully. The goal is to match the boat's characteristics to the engine by using a propeller that will allow the engine to attain (or remain slightly below) the engine manufacturer's specification for WOT (wide open throttle) rpm. That match can be made with any number of different props whose design will affect many other aspects of the boat's performance, such as acceleration out of the hole, smoothness of operation, and top speed. The result may be that the standard propeller is a good match for the engine, but its performance fails to meet the owner's needs in other ways. Those needs can be met by changing props, but the match with the engine at WOT has to be maintained.

Propeller performance can be affected in a number of ways: changing the pitch, increasing the number of blades, opting for a different design (changing the shape of the blades), and by changing the diameter. The first, changing the pitch, is the most common and most predictable. A general rule of thumb is that a 1" change in pitch will result in a change of 200 engine rpm. Props with more blades can deliver more bite and run more smoothly. Changes in basic design can enhance particular areas of performance, such as top speed. Changing the diameter is a less likely option because of space constraints imposed by the boat, outboard motor or outdrive.

Propeller technology has come a long way in 150 years, but the dizzying number of propeller choices means that owners looking to upgrade their boat's performance need to be more careful than ever. The powerplant or boat manufacturer's recommendations are a good place to start looking for information that will help make the right choice. Dealers should be happy to provide manufacturers' literature showing performance data and comparison results. Major manufacturers and distributors also have a service whereby they ask you to fill out a questionnaire about your boat and how you use it, and will help you make the decision. Beyond that, the most important requirement is that you know how you want to tailor your boat's performance and what trade-offs you're willing to accept to attain your goal. If you're looking for increased top speed, for example, you may have to give up a bit coming out of the hole, or vice versa. Deciding what you want up front will make the whole process easier.

Today's propeller technology will take over from there.

Chapter Eight
Trim Tabs
Control to the Max

We've all seen it at one time or another — a boat, plowing through the water with its transom tucked down almost below water level and its bow riding so high that the skipper has to stand on tip-toes just to see where he's going. There are three possible reasons for the situation. He has no trim tabs, he doesn't know how to use trim tabs, or he's filming a commercial for a trim tab company.

Trim tabs are one of the most useful devices you can put on a boat, but many boaters aren't fully aware of their many functions and advantages. Even venerable *Chapman's* has remarkably little to say about their role in boat handling.

For the few who haven't been exposed to them, powerboat trim tabs are metal flaps hinged at or near the trailing edge of a boat's hull that can be tilted down or drawn back up by a hydraulic cylinder or other mechanism whose action is controlled remotely from the helm. They are first cousins to an airplane's ailerons or wing flaps. When the boat is under way, the tabs can be rotated down at an angle to provide increased lift at the stern. The greater the angle, the greater the lift. They can be used to great advantage on almost any small- to medium-size boat with a planing or semi-displacement hull. Most modern trim tab systems feature a completely self-contained, electrically driven hydraulic pump and fluid reservoir that greatly reduces the chance of messy leaks and is quite simple to maintain. Just check the fluid level occasionally and keep the tabs free of debris and encrustation.

The most common use for trim tabs is to correct the bow-up situation described earlier. The problem can be caused by loading the boat too heavily at the stern or, more often, by the need or desire to go faster than displacement speed, but yet not fast enough to get up on plane. The boat is permanently "on the hump" — pushing a hill of water in that transitional attitude just before it goes on plane. Rotating the tabs down, as shown in Figure 1, will provide the lift needed to drop the bow and put the boat in a more manageable, safe and comfortable attitude while running at reduced speed.

UNCORRECTED

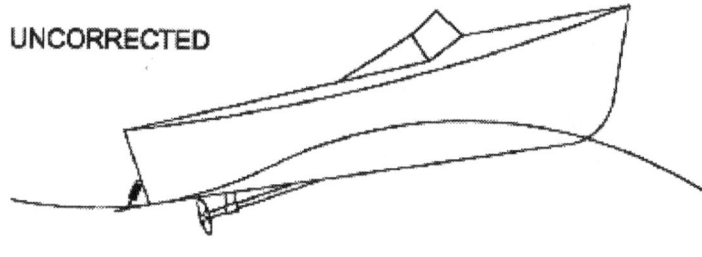

TRIM TABS DEPLOYED

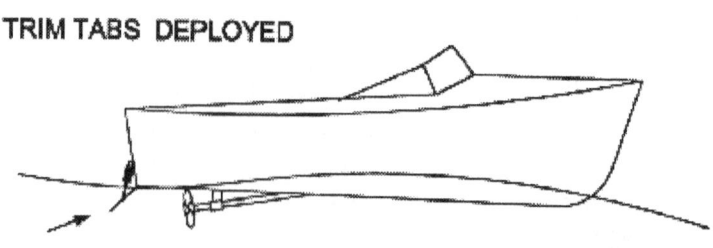

Figure 8-1

Using trim tabs to correct running angle.

The tabs can also be used to keep the bow down when heading into a chop. Without them, the buoyant bow may try to ride up and over each wave, allowing the chop to slam on the bottom, making for a very rough ride and a loss of directional stability. By using the tabs properly, the bow can be forced down so that it knifes through the chop, rather than riding over it.

Knowledgeable owners of outboard-powered and stern-drive boats will tell you their motor or drive can be tilted down and in toward the transom to provide the same effect as trim tabs. They're correct up to a point, but that function is mainly intended to provide efficient trim at planing speeds, so the effect is rarely as pronounced as it would be with trim tabs. A small boat with a V8 stern drive has much of its weight concentrated aft, and the direction of force from the angled drive is at a considerable mechanical disadvantage when it comes to providing the lift required to get the boat in proper trim, especially at low speeds.

UNCORRECTED

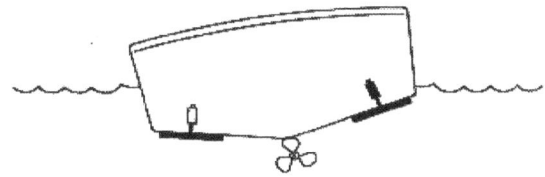

TAB DEPLOYED

Figure 8-2
Using trim tabs to correct listing.

Even in those instances where the tilt adjustment is up to the job, the tabs still have one important advantage: they can be operated independently to compensate for potentially dangerous side-to-side imbalances. Whether the list is caused by improper loading or by external conditions (such as current or wind coming in on the beam), the tabs can be used to trim the boat back into a level attitude. As shown in Figure 2, a list to port can be trimmed out by lowering the port tab to increase lift on that side.

The controls for trim tabs can be confusing and may require some concentration at first, but they soon become second nature. Most are comprised of a set of switches, either a pair of rocker switches or a square group of four buttons, but there are joystick controls too. The confusion can come from the fact that the starboard switches control the port tab and vice versa. To make matters worse, the actions of the controls are often labeled in terms of bow position, when you're thinking about the position of the stern. Getting the stern up requires you to push the bow down, and dropping the port bow means raising the starboard quarter. Once the initial unfamiliarity is overcome, most boaters find that the tabs become an important part of their everyday routine and they wonder how they ever managed without them.

Trim tabs are a very useful accessory, but they have some disadvantages to keep in mind, too. Using them to maintain fore-and-aft trim at intermediate speeds may mean your boat isn't running in its most efficient manner. The resulting reduction in fuel economy can be made even worse by the drag the tabs produce because the greater the tab angle, the more drag will result. In salt water, they're another piece of metal to factor into your electrolysis-protection scheme. And if your boat has a swim platform, you'll need to warn swimmers of the presence of the tabs to prevent injury from their sharp edges.

A more serious problem can arise from trying to back up with trim tabs deployed. Their effect will be just the opposite of going forward; they'll pull the stern down, make the boat plow into the water and impair your ability to steer. In a worst case, a boat with a low or notched transom could even take on some water in the process, so it's important to remember to retract the tabs before reversing. And finally, it's important to insure that tabs are fully retracted to prevent them from being damaged during launching or hauling operations.

Builders who don't include trim tabs as standard equipment on their boats usually offer them as a relatively inexpensive option. Adding them to an existing boat can cost less than $500 if you install them yourself, and most of the kits available through marine suppliers are pre-engineered for easy installation. The hydraulic pump along with its control valve and fluid reservoir is often a single unit that can be mounted to the inside of the transom or on a stringer. The control panel and its connecting cable are often set up to simply plug together, thus eliminating complicated electrical wiring, and there are a minimum number of holes to be drilled in the hull, so there are few excuses for going without them. Trim tabs will make you a better skipper and render your boating much more enjoyable. You'll wonder how you ever managed without them.

Modern Boatworks -- By David S. Yetman

Chapter Nine
Surviving A Mechanical Emergency

We were rafted up about 50 feet off the beach with several other boats when we noticed a boater in much shallower water who was having trouble starting his engine. When we asked if he needed a hand, he waded out toward us and said he thought he had a clogged fuel filter and asked if we had a wrench that might help him remove it.

"Sure!" said my raft neighbor Dick. He disappeared into the cuddy cabin of his 24-footer and emerged a minute later with a shiny filter wrench. The other boater was amazed but gratefully headed back to his boat with his prize, only to return a few minutes later to say that it was too large to fit his filter.

"No problem," Dick replied, and promptly appeared with an equally shiny filter wrench of the next smaller size.

"My God," said his wife, rolling her eyes, "he has everything down there. There's no room to move!"

If you also feel obliged to carry every tool and spare part that the experts say you absolutely shouldn't leave shore without, you'd need to move up to a small freighter to have room for them. Preparing yourself to handle mechanical emergencies is smart and an important part of your responsibility to your passengers,

Modern Boatworks -- By David S. Yetman

but you shouldn't need a stevedore and a dock crane to get your tool kit and spares aboard. Your ability to handle a mechanical emergency depends on having a kit assembled with you, your boat and the way you use it in mind, not on a huge array of tools. It's also important to know your boat. You should read, or at least scan the engine manual so you know what's in it and keep it on the boat for reference.

The way you use your boat and where you use it are the first considerations. If chasing bluefish 20 miles offshore is your favorite pastime, you'll want to have a more extensive kit than your neighbor who spends Sunday afternoons bass fishing on an inland pond. He can paddle his broken boat to shore and go home. You can't. If you keep your boat at a slip some distance from home, you'll probably want a more complete kit, even if you keep it in your car rather than on board. Another consideration is the practical limitation on what you can accomplish while helplessly bobbing around out there. You may be able to replace a belt or water pump impeller, or tighten something that's loosened up, but you're not going do anything about a broken timing chain or a blown head gasket, so you might as well leave the gear puller and torque wrench at home.

The boat and its condition should influence your choices, too. Twin engines can help ensure that you'll limp back on one unless you have a fuel problem, but they double the number of spare filters you'll need to carry. If your boat is older, remember that it may suffer more problems than a new one. And keep its history in mind. If it likes to chew up generator belts, or if a particular part on your outboard has been a problem, for example, make sure you always have one in your spares kit.

You (or more specifically, your capabilities) will also dictate what you carry in your tool kit. If your mechanical abilities are limited, the number of repairs you can do and therefore the number of tools you'll need will be fewer. Even so, you should still carry basic tools and spares, and most importantly, some means of calling for assistance when you have a problem.

Basic tools are screwdrivers, pliers, wrenches and cutting devices. Make sure the wrenches match your boat. Modern engines mostly use metric fasteners. Older ones may have American (fractional) ones or a combination of the two, depending on who manufactured the engine's accessories. It's also a good idea to carry an adjustable wrench that will fit the largest nut on board (usually the prop nut). Unless your pond is very small and you live next door, the following should be included in the most basic tool kit:

#1 and #2 Phillips screwdrivers
small, medium and large flat-bladed screwdrivers
small slip-joint pliers
large ChanneLock pliers
needle-nose pliers
wire-cutting pliers
combination wrenches (box and open-end)
large adjustable wrench (or a prop-nut wrench)
knife with both serrated and straight blades
spool of mechanic's wire
roll of quality duct tape

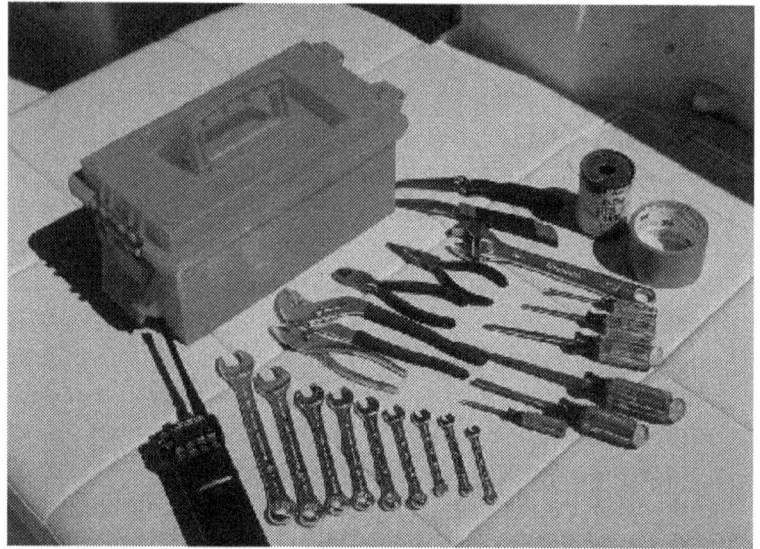

Figure 9-1

Contents of a basic mechanical emergency tool kit.

All of the above will fit into a small tackle box, or better still, an inexpensive waterproof box that doesn't take up limited dry storage space. You may be tempted to settle for one of those miracle devices that hang on your belt and fold out into thirty different "tools." They're handy, especially if you have nothing else, but keep in mind that serious work requires real tools.

Other tools you may choose to add to the basics will be dictated by the needs of your boat and personal preference. A set of socket wrenches, allen wrenches, nut drivers for hose clamps, files, an awl or even a tapered reamer can come in handy. If you use your boat in an area where fuel contamination is a problem, you'll want to have the proper tools for filter changes too. And don't fall into the trap of filling your kit with worn-out, cast-off or inexpensive tools. Your safety could depend on their usefulness, and cheap tools can cost you dearly.

Modern Boatworks -- By David S. Yetman

Another part of being prepared is spare parts. They should be limited to what you can realistically replace within the limitations described earlier, but you should carry spares. If you use your boat in an area where rocks or a hard bottom are prevalent, a spare prop is a necessity. Replacements for each drive belt are a good idea, as are a water pump impeller, parts you've historically had problems with, and spark plugs, points, condenser and a coil if your boat doesn't have electronic ignition. If you have any doubts, talk with the dealer or mechanic who sold or serviced your boat and get their advice.

It's impossible to be prepared for everything that could possibly happen, so don't forget the most important tool of all: a device that will allow you to call for assistance when all else fails. Costs have dropped dramatically, so there's no reason to be unable to call for help. Whether a marine VHF (usually the best choice for offshore use) or a cell phone or CB in areas where they are more likely to provide reliable communication, every boat should have one. Now that my friend Dick has moved up to a much larger boat, I'll bet he has two of each.

Modern Boatworks -- By David S. Yetman

Modern Boatworks -- By David S. Yetman

Chapter Ten
Electronic Ignition Systems

Many boat owners aren't old enough to remember the frustration and inconvenience of the "points, plugs and condenser" tune-up routine that everyone had to put up with just a few short years ago. During that era we felt quite fortunate if we could drive more than a few thousand miles or use our boats for a full season without having to replace that trio of problematic parts, then laboriously adjust the point gap, lubricate the distributor cam and set the engine timing. Those who have been through it have been lulled into forgetting by modern powerplants that will literally go for years without a tune-up. Much of the technology that has made the transition possible can be found in electronic ignition systems, but reliability and freedom from maintenance are only part of the story.

The basic parts of a traditional ignition system were a high-voltage coil to supply energy to the spark plugs, a set of contact points that acted like a switch to turn the electricity to the coil on and off, a distributor to direct the output to the spark plugs, and a condenser to protect the points from the coil's surge. One of the two points was solidly mounted, while the other was connected to a pivot and fitted with a phenolic block that rode on a cam attached to the distributor shaft so that each lobe would lift the block and cause the points to open. When the points were closed, power would flow into the coil, building up an electric field. When the points opened, interrupting the flow of electricity to the coil, the field would collapse, sending its energy to the spark plug.

The system worked well when it worked, but the high current carried by the points pitted their contact surfaces, which reduced their conductivity and affected coil performance. And the cam follower would wear down, changing ignition timing, reducing the point opening, producing arcs between the points and causing still more pitting or complete point closure, which stopped the engine cold. The ignition system was a high-maintenance item, but in retrospect, an even more important drawback was its lack of flexibility. Once ignition timing had been set through a series of mechanical adjustments, it could only be varied in response to engine speed or throttle opening because it was mechanically controlled by a centrifugal-advance mechanism for the former and by a vacuum-operated advance for the latter, both housed within the distributor.

Electronic ignition systems would change all of that. The revolutionary benefits of electronic ignition are the result of two seemingly simple changes. They eliminated the need for contact points and provided the opportunity to break the mechanical control link to the engine.

In an electronic system, points are replaced by magnetic sensors or solid-state devices such as Hall-effect sensors or optical detectors, all of which operate without coming in contact with a moving part, thus eliminating the wear problem associated with the points' cam follower. The lobes of the distributor cam are replaced by tiny magnets, one for each cylinder. As each rotates past the sensor, it triggers an output pulse from the sensor. There's no arcing or pitting to worry about because there are no contacts. Solid-state devices operate at very low power levels, however, so their output is quite weak. Magnetic and Hall-effect devices, for example, emit only a tiny pulse of electricity when actuated by a magnet. Ordinarily, the pulse would be too weak to accomplish anything or even be detected, but when fed into an amplifier circuit, it can be strengthened and used to control much more demanding tasks such as firing an ignition coil.

In its simplest form, electronic ignition simply replaces contact points with a solid-state module that contains both the sensor and its amplifier. The module is retrofitted to the engine's existing distributor, so the system still relies on mechanical advance and vacuum-advance mechanisms.

On the face of it, the need to be coupled with electronics would seem to be a liability, but it turns out to be an important asset because it allows ignition-system control to be integrated into the electronic engine controller or engine control module (EEC or ECM), which is also used to control the engine's fuel injection system. This is the fullest implementation of electronic ignition because it allows ignition timing to be varied by instructions from the control system instead of a rigid mechanical link. The result is intelligent electronic control of engine operation.

In distributor-less ignition systems such as those on some outboards, the EEC uses sensors that read directly from the crankshaft or some other rotating component mechanically connected to the engine. The sensors, wherever they are located, supply information about the position of the moving components of the engine that affect timing. That information, combined with the rest of the inputs to the EEC (See Chapter 2), allow its computer to determine the optimum operating

Modern Boatworks -- By David S. Yetman

conditions for the engine and make adjustments to fuel injection and ignition-system functions to provide the most efficient operation.

If the EEC's sensors detect engine knocking, for example, it can retard the timing just enough to prevent it, then return it to normal when the load eases or the quality of the fuel improves. Ignition timing is no longer determined on the basis of engine speed and throttle opening; it is adjusted to suit a broad range of operating conditions that have been detected by other sensors. The adjustments can be made as often as 20 times per second, assuring that ignition timing is always matched to the demands of its current environment. The result is increased power, reduced emissions, better fuel economy, greater reliability and freedom from maintenance.

Like electronic fuel injection, electronic ignition systems have delivered benefits to users that were unimaginable 30 years ago, but their individual contributions would have been of significantly less value if it were not for their ability to become part of a larger, computer-controlled system. As much as we admire the throaty growl of the engines beneath our decks, the computer is the real star of the story behind today's powerful, reliable, economical power plants.

Modern Boatworks -- By David S. Yetman

Chapter Eleven
Inverters
AC In A DC World

Most of us run into a conundrum very early in our boating experience: we need to run an electrical device on board, but are stymied by the lack of AC power. Basic electrical systems on boats are DC, yet most common appliances and tools require AC. As frustrating as the incompatibility may be, there is a logical reason for it, and a number of solutions are available to help you to bridge the gap.

The defining difference between the two types of power is that direct current always flows smoothly in the same direction, where alternating current changes direction 60 times per second (or 50 in Europe). While AC is the standard household and industrial-power medium, a significant number of modern conveniences such as radios, TVs, computers, navigation devices and nearly all control and monitoring systems require pure DC. Every one that plugs into household AC accommodates its need with a rectifier circuit that changes AC to DC for internal use.

There are powerful reasons for maintaining both AC and DC systems and putting up with the constant need to change one to the other to suit particular situations.

Modern Boatworks -- *By David S. Yetman*

AC has many important attributes. It's far easier to generate and transmit at very high voltages over long distances and can be stepped up or down in voltage with use of inexpensive transformers. It's safer to use, especially at high voltages, because it's not as prone to arcing and burning as DC, so devices like motors, heaters, air-conditioners and stoves that require lots of power are safer, easier to build and use with AC.

DC has its own attributes. Devices like the ones listed above simply will not operate on anything but DC. It's not a matter of choice in design; it's governed by the laws of physics. Transistors, integrated circuits and computer chips run on DC, period. The other important feature, though, is that DC can be generated and stored in batteries; AC cannot. Mobile devices as small as a flashlight or as large as a yacht depend on stored energy and that means DC.

Figure 11-1

Creature comforts such as coffee-makers and microwave ovens require on-board AC power.

The incompatibility between electrical systems is normally invisible to users. The only time the difference becomes a problem is when you have one but need the other. Converting AC to DC is by far the easier of the tasks because AC is usually present in higher voltages than the DC requirement, and the circuitry needed to reduce the voltage and rectify it to DC is simple, inexpensive and doesn't put a great strain on the AC system. Going from DC to AC is more difficult. In fact, in situations where large amounts of AC power are required on a continual basis, conversion from an available DC source is often impractical and unwieldy. The builders of most large vessels equip them with gasoline- or diesel-power AC generators connected to on-board AC wiring, identical to a household system. While this is an expensive solution, it offers many advantages, including independence from shore-side facilities and the ability to recharge on-board batteries from the AC system.

Figure 11-2
Courtesy of Statpower Technologies Corp.

A thousand watt inverter.

The need for occasional AC power on smaller boats is usually filled with the use of less-expensive DC-to-AC inverters. For much of their history, inverters were crude, inefficient, weighty devices that made boaters think twice about using them, but the technology has improved to the point that their use is growing steadily. Modern solid-state inverters are smaller, lighter and more reliable than ever. For occasional use to power a small radio or TV, a portable unit that plugs into a cigarette lighter outlet can supply up to 250 watts of AC power if the outlet is fused appropriately. For more demanding applications, a permanently installed unit will do the job, but in spite of modern technology, inverters still have their own set of liabilities.

Figure 11-3
Even a small, 400W inverter should be mounted as close to the battery as possible.

The primary drawback is the need to produce 110 volts AC from only 12 volts DC. Look at an inverter whose output is rated at 500 watts, for example. Five hundred watts of power at 110 volts means an output-current drain of about 4.5 amps. Assuming that the inverter is a good one and 90-percent efficient, it would draw 555 watts from the 12-volt source at maximum output. At 12 volts, 555 watts equates to 46 amps of current. By the same accounting, a 1,000-watt inverter could draw nearly 100 amps. These are levels of current that demand great respect and attention during wiring selection, installation and maintenance because they can cause severe problems if improperly handled (the most dangerous of which is the potential for fire).

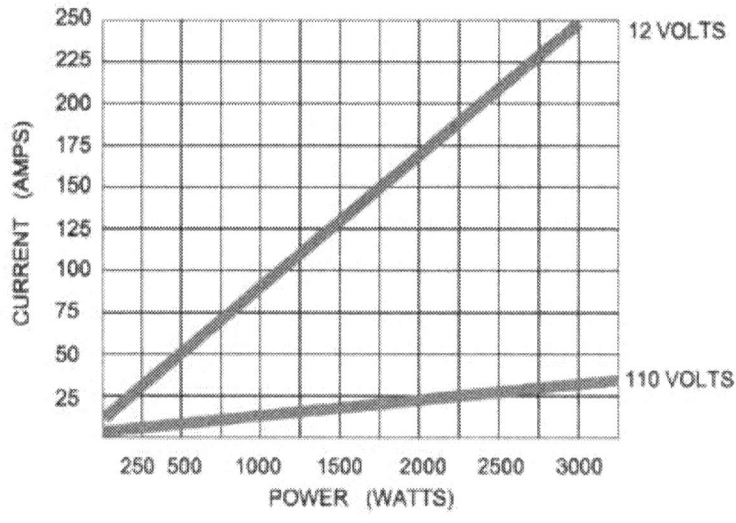

Figure 11-4

Electrical current comparison between 12 volts DC and 110 volts AC.

If the inverter is connected to the battery with a wire of insufficient size, the wire will heat up in response to the overload even if all its connections are tight. If it's sufficiently overloaded, it can get red-hot. Using the correct wire size is a must, but only the first step. As mentioned above, DC is quite prone to arcing and will do so quite readily across a loose connection. Temperatures within the arc can reach 2,000_, more than enough to melt insulation, burn through a bulkhead or even melt metal. (See Chapter 13 for more information on wiring.)

A proper installation will place the inverter as close to the batteries as possible, use the input-wire size recommended by the manufacturer (or larger if possible), and all connections will be made with crimp or soldered lugs at the wire termination. If the inverter doesn't have its own input fuse, you should provide one (or a circuit breaker) between it and the battery. For larger inverters, it's not practical to run the input wiring all the way to the boat's circuit breaker panel because the resistance of the excess wire will cause a voltage drop, and most breaker panels won't handle high currents anyway. Once the installation is complete, include a thorough inspection of its connections as part of your weekly maintenance routine.

Another drawback of using an inverter is its ability to drain your batteries flat in a very short time. Installing one on a boat with just a single battery is an invitation for trouble. They should be run from an auxiliary battery that can be isolated from the rest of the system during use. Some inverters are designed to shut themselves off when the power source drops below 11 volts or so, but at that point the battery may not have enough reserve to get you up and running if it's your only one.

Finally, if you are going to power a TV or other equipment that may be sensitive about input power, you need to be aware of one more difference in inverters. Inexpensive models may not produce a perfect AC output waveform, causing some noise or instability to appear on screen. They will also prevent some types of AC devices from operating as efficiently as intended, producing excess heat in the process. These irritants can be avoided by making sure the output waveform of the inverter is sinusoidal. Manufacturers' data will specify "true sine wave" or "fully sinusoidal" for the latter, where older designs or less expensive units will be listed as "quasi-sinusoidal" or "modified sine wave." As with everything in life, be prepared to spend a bit more for the good stuff.

    Modern inverters can be the perfect answer to the need for occasional AC power. They are reliable and comparatively inexpensive but must be chosen, installed, maintained and used properly. Under the right conditions, they are an accessory that makes life aboard much more enjoyable and convenient.

Electrical Terms

AC: alternating current; reverses direction of flow (60 times per second in the U.S.)

Amp: an abbreviation for ampere, the unit of measure for electrical flow or current. The higher the current, the more power is delivered at a specific voltage.
      (AMPS = WATTS ÷ VOLTS)

DC: direct current; flows smoothly in one direction only.

Modern Boatworks -- By David S. Yetman

Volt: unit of measure for electrical potential; higher voltage will overcome resistance more easily and provide greater power at a specific current.
(VOLTS = WATTS ÷ AMPS)

Voltage Drop: loss of voltage resulting from resistance in the delivery system (usually wire).
(VOLTAGE DROP = AMPS x OHMS)

Watt: unit of measure for electrical power.
(WATTS = VOLTS x AMPS)

Chapter Twelve
Shore-Power Systems

There was a time when only large, expensive boats were equipped with shore-power systems that allow AC appliances and equipment to be used on board. Now it's not uncommon to see them on boats as small as 22 or 24 feet. Unfortunately, not all boats are so equipped, and those that are don't always have outlets where you need them, but either of those situations is relatively easy to correct.

Installing a basic shore-power system or expanding an existing one doesn't require a great deal of specialized knowledge or equipment, but the task should be approached with a healthy respect for the potential danger of 110 volts AC and the damage that can result from improper wiring or sloppy workmanship.

Before you decide to work on any on-board electrical system, read this chapter completely and the chapter that follows. Following three basic rules will help to ensure success and safety: 1) Gain at least a basic understanding of the electrical circuit you are working with; 2) Use only wire and components that have been specifically designed and manufactured for marine use; 3) Inspect and test your work thoroughly before you power up the system.

Modern Boatworks -- By David S. Yetman

Electrical Basics

Figure 1 shows a wiring diagram of a basic shore-power system. The power comes in through the shore-power inlet plug and goes directly to the distribution panel, a central location for circuit breakers or fuses. Circuit breakers are more common than fuses in AC circuits because they can be reset after being tripped (a fuse just burns out) and can also be used as a switch to turn circuits on and off. Individual circuits, each protected by a circuit breaker, fan out from the distribution panel. The circuits may serve one or more outlets or be dedicated to a specific appliance or piece of equipment.

Another protective device that should be used liberally is the ground fault interrupter (GFI), which senses excess leakage of current to ground and quickly shuts the circuit off before damage or injury can occur. Leakage may be the result of an equipment failure or even someone in the early stages of getting an electrical shock. If the GFI is placed closest to the current source, it will also protect the rest of the outlets in the circuit. The GFI can be built into an outlet as shown in Figure1 or may be a stand-alone device mounted and connected back at the distribution panel. The outlet version is handier, since it has buttons for testing and resetting the circuit after being tripped.

A basic 110-volt shore-power system is connected using three wires, often referred to as "legs." The hot wire always has black insulation and is the wire that is interrupted by a switch or circuit breaker. The neutral wire has white insulation and is not switched in normal use. The ground wire will have green insulation (or green and yellow under European regulations) and is never interrupted or switched because it is the safety wire. All three may be daisy-chained from one outlet to the next but should only make connections at a screw terminal and never be spliced in mid-route. When connecting to outlets or directly to equipment, the black wire is always attached to a brass-colored screw and white wires to silver-colored screws. The terminal for the green ground wire will have a hex-head screw (all the others are round) attached directly into a metal frame bracket or painted green.

Distribution panels are used in conjunction with insulated terminal strips, one for each leg, that provide a secure method of attaching multiple wires to the same electrical point. As Figure 1 shows, the black wires always connect to other black wires, white to white and green to green. No current flows through the system until a load is plugged into a receptacle, completing a loop circuit comprised of the hot wire, load, neutral wire and the power company generator some miles away. The ground wire is not part of the loop and carries no current under normal conditions.

Adding To a System

The four most important things to consider when planning to add to an existing system are: 1) where the wiring will be routed; 2) where and how to mount additional outlet(s); 3) how to tie the addition into the system; and 4) insuring that the addition will not overload the system or some part of it, causing a safety hazard.

Finding ways to route new wiring on a boat can be the most difficult part of the job, but it is where good planning will make a huge difference.

Modern Boatworks -- By David S. Yetman

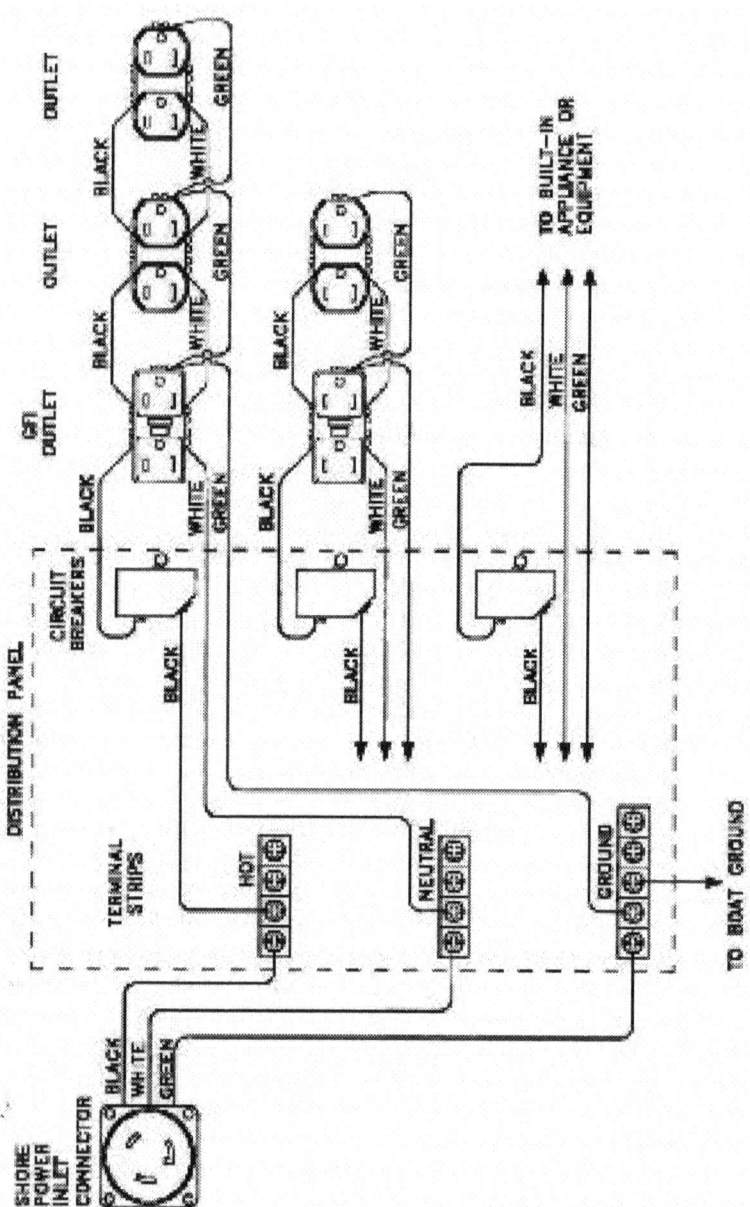

Figure 12-1

Wiring diagram of a typical shore power system.

The easiest way is to install new wiring along the path of existing wiring or plumbing wherever possible. Drill holes only as a last resort. Unlike DC wiring, AC circuits rarely suffer because of excess length, so a circuitous routing will do no harm. The wiring route should avoid shafts, control rods, steering cables or anything else that moves or chafes. It should be as far as possible from engine exhaust systems and be as high as possible in bilge areas. Use a rigid wire "snake" to drag the wire through difficult spots, but be sure that the system is unplugged from the shore receptacle and that the main switch of the DC system is off before using a metal snake to probe in blind spots.

Additions such as stoves or refrigerators may be designed to be wired directly into the system, bypassing the need for an outlet and plug, but they will still need the protection of a circuit breaker or fuse. Such devices should not be added to existing circuits that serve other outlets or devices. They will require another circuit breaker or fuse. If the existing panel doesn't have a spare or room for another breaker, it may be more cost-effective to add another small panel with two or three breaker positions. The power to the auxiliary panel can be taken directly from the terminal strips of the main panel.

A number of options exist for mounting additional outlets. If there is no possible access to the back of the outlet once it has been installed, the outlet can be safely mounted directly into the panel or bulkhead. Mounting an outlet without using a box will require an accurately sized wall cutout that is as close to the size of the outlet body as possible. An oversize cutout may remove material that the mounting screws would normally screw into.

If there's even a remote possibility that someone could come in contact with the back of an outlet, it must

Modern Boatworks -- By David S. Yetman

be mounted in the type of wall box used in home installations or provided with some type of cover that will prevent accidental contact. One type of plastic box that is widely available has two integral clamps that will hold it in place permanently. Once the box is inserted into the rectangular hole cut in the bulkhead, a few turns with a screwdriver will draw the clamps up against the back of the wall to secure the box. All standard boxes have holes to accept an outlet or switch and faceplate. Outlets mounted in unprotected areas such as the helm or cockpit should be mounted in a standard box and fitted with an outdoor-type faceplate equipped with gasketed, spring-loaded covers.

If the addition does not require its own circuit breaker, it must be tied to an existing circuit. The easiest point to connect it will be to the outlet at the end of a string of outlets. As shown at the top of Figure 1, all of the screw terminals of outlets in the daisy chain are used except for the last one, which has a pair of unused terminals. This is the best place to tie in an addition. The alternative is to double up wires on other terminals, which may be difficult in the confines of a box and be a safety hazard because they are more likely to loosen up.

If your boat did not come with a list or diagram showing which outlets and accessories are connected to the individual breakers, it's a good idea to make one before you add to the system. Knowing how many outlets are on one circuit and how they're likely to be used will help you make intelligent decisions about additional outlets. If you have an appliance whose current draw is not marked, you can easily determine its needs by dividing its wattage by 110 (volts). A 1,000-watt toaster, for example, will draw 1,000 ÷ 110 or 9.1 amps. Two such appliances used simultaneously would overload a circuit served by a 15-amp circuit breaker.

Any work you perform on an electrical system should be followed by a thorough inspection and test before you apply power to it. The first part should be a visual inspection to ensure there are no bare wires; that black wires are connected only to other black wires etc., and that all connections are secure. This should be followed by an electrical test to look for short circuits. This can be done with a continuity tester or a multi-tester. (See Chapter 17 for more info on inexpensive multi-testers and their use.) Double-check that the shore-power system is disconnected (not just shut off) and that all circuit breakers are off before you begin testing. Insert the test probes into the receptacles of a new outlet so that they touch the metal contacts and ensure that there is no continuity between any two of the three contacts. (Continuity between any of them would indicate a potentially dangerous short circuit, although the problem could be anywhere in the circuit being tested, not necessarily in that outlet.) Finally, power up the system and check to see that all outlets of the modified circuit are functional.

Installing a New System

Installing a new shore-power system involves all of the same issues and caveats discussed above, but with the additional tasks of installing an inlet connector and a distribution panel and running wire where there is none to begin with.

Inlet connectors, distribution panels and power cords that have been specifically designed for marine use are relatively expensive items, so you may be tempted to search for lower-cost alternatives. Don't do so. The potential for personal injury and property damage is too great to be traded for a few dollars saved. Even if your system will be just a single outlet tucked away in the cuddy cabin, it should have all of the protective safety features of a larger system.

The distribution panel should be mounted in an area that is accessible, protected from the elements and offering clear paths for bringing wiring to it. Its location should also be chosen with an eye to keeping the distance between it and the inlet connector as short and direct as possible. Although most dockside power outlets will have their own circuit breakers or fuses, their condition and reliability should not be assumed. This means that the wiring between them and your circuit breakers is essentially unprotected (unfused), so it should be kept short and be well protected from chafe or damage.

The inlet connector should also be mounted in a protected place if possible. Although properly designed connectors have gasketed covers and their mating plugs are well sealed, keeping them dry and out of the way is a good idea. The wiring between the inlet connector and the distribution panel carries all of the power for your system, so its wire size is very important. For a 30-amp system (adequate for most small boats), the wire size should be no smaller than 10 gauge and larger if possible, especially if the distance between connector and panel is greater than 10 or 12 feet. A good practice in this situation is to use the largest wire size that the connector is designed to accept. The final consideration in installing a new system is to ensure that the ground leg is connected to the boat's ground (DC negative). The connection should be made using the same size wire as that between the inlet connector and the panel.

Working on shore-power systems should not be taken lightly. Do not attempt it if some aspect of it is unclear. Do not inspect, test or work on any AC electrical system that has not been disconnected from its power source. Any discussion of more extensive, high-power shore-power systems has been purposely omitted from this chapter in the strong belief that such systems and their increased complexity and potential for hazards should be left in the hands of professionals who have the experience and specialized tools to do the job properly.

Modern Boatworks -- By David S. Yetman

Chapter Thirteen
Wiring Basics

Satisfying the electrical needs of a boat presents some unique challenges. Conditions such as copious amounts of moisture (often laden with salt), vibration, physical shock and irregular use result in electrical systems that require specialized components, careful construction and vigilant maintenance.

Any repair or addition that doesn't meet the material or workmanship standards for marine systems is a weak link that will almost certainly develop into a problem at some point. Beyond insuring that any components you add are specifically designed for the marine environment, the three main wiring considerations are wire type, proper connections and wire gauge (diameter).

Wire Type

Electrical wire designed for marine use is always stranded, not solid, and is constructed of multiple copper strands that have been individually tin-plated before being wound into wire. This is true for both AC and DC applications. Stranded wire is more flexible than solid wire, which makes it nearly impervious to the vibration that can cause unsupported solid wire to break very quickly. Tin plating prevents corrosion of the copper wire and makes it easier to solder. The best marine wire will also have high-temperature (105C / 220F) plastic insulation to provide continued protection if it gets hot.

Marine wire is available singly or in cables of two (duplex, triplex, etc.) to as many as eight conductors. Multi-conductor cable is much easier to use for construction or additions because it only has to be snaked through once, and the fact that the wires are bundled together means that connections are easier to make. The use of cable instead of individual wires also results in a much neater installation.

Connections

Because it is stranded, marine wire should always be connected to screw terminals with the use of insulated, crimp-on ring connectors. Although they add cost and require the use of special crimping pliers, crimp-on terminals provide the kind of safe, secure, mechanically robust connections that are necessary in marine environments. The crimp captures the wire with great force, and the ring end will keep the wire connected to the terminal even if the screw loosens up. Ring connectors are defined by the maximum wire size and by the maximum screw size they will accept. The wire size should be matched as closely as possible to insure a strong, reliable connection.

Two types of ring connectors are available in most marine stores. The most common one has a tubular receptacle which gets crimped onto the wire and a simple plastic sleeve to insulate the crimp. The second has the same type of receptacle but has a longer insulating sleeve meant to be crimped onto the insulation of the wire too. This second type captures the insulation of the wire and provides a more secure junction (and can be required in some applications governed by CE [European] rules), but requires a more expensive, dual-action crimping tool. The simpler connectors do an adequate job, and the crimping pliers required to attach them are available at marine or hardware stores for less than $10. Additional insulation can be added to meet special needs with a layer of shrinkable tubing or electrical tape around the shank of the connector.

Wiring added to a boat should have sufficient length to allow it to be tied to existing wiring or other supports along its path to keep it from flopping around or chafing in route. Leave enough length at its ends to make it convenient to connect and ensure there will be no strain on the connections. This is especially important where the wire will end in an electrical outlet box or exit through a hole in a bulkhead.

Wire Size

Choosing the correct type of wire and providing it with ring connectors is easy. Determining the correct size of wire is less straightforward, mainly because of the number of variables to be considered, but it is important to get it right. There are slightly different standards for AC wiring, which tends to be high-voltage (above 100V) and DC wiring, which is usually used in low voltage (below 50V) circuits.

Wire size is described by a gauge number specified by several competing but very similar standards. The most common is AWG (American Wire Gauge). The larger the number, the smaller the wire diameter. The smaller the wire diameter, the less current it can carry.

The main considerations in determining the capacity of a given wire size are voltage drop over the length of the wire, which is caused by the natural resistance of the wire, and the heat generated by the energy lost in overcoming the resistance (usually discussed in terms of temperature rise). In a worst-case scenario, excess current drawn through an undersize wire can result in a loss of power or a very hot wire. In extreme cases, the power may not be sufficient to run the device drawing the current and the wire could get hot enough to be a fire hazard.

In every instance where the theoretically appropriate wire for a DC circuit is sought, the first considerations will be how much power loss you can tolerate and how much heat you can dissipate. Most wire-size tables for marine use will list the maximum allowable current for a given wire size under optimum conditions, i.e. a single wire in air (not bundled in a cable) and not in an engine compartment The notes to the table will then explain that the maximum current for that wire should be de-rated by 15 percent in an engine compartment by an additional 30 percent if it is bundled with two other wires and up to 50 percent if bundled with seven or more wires. A #16 wire, for example, is rated at 25 amps under optimum conditions in the ABYC-based DC chart below, but could only be used at 10.6 amps in a large bundle in an engine compartment. The main reason for the need to de-rate the current-carrying capacity of the wire is the reduction of heat dissipation that takes place when the wire is tied up in a bundle or cable or run in a hot environment.

In reality, there is rarely any overriding reason to use the absolutely smallest possible wire size, so extreme operating conditions and their attending dangers can be avoided by simply choosing conservatively. In the case mentioned above, 10 amps is a safe, conservative rating for #16 wire. Smaller wire sizes (below #18) can be damaged or broken easily and so should not be used unless they are part of a commercially manufactured cable such as that supplied with electronic instruments.

MAXIMUM ALLOWABLE DC CURRENT (AMPS)

AWG WIRE GAUGE	MAXIMUM ABYC RATING	AGGRESSIVE 10% VOLTAGE DROP @ 20FT	CONSERVATIVE 3% VOLTAGE DROP @ 20FT
#16	25A	18A	6A
#14	35A	28A	8A
#12	45A	38A	11A
#10	60A	56A	18A
#8	80A	80A	28A
#6	120A	120A	44A
#4	160A	160A	70A
#2	210A	210A	110A
#1	245A	245A	140A

Figure 13-1

Because AC power is delivered at higher, more efficient voltages, considerations of voltage drop or power loss due to the resistance and length of the wires are not as important as they are in low-voltage DC wiring. The result is that wire size for AC shore-power systems can be determined reliably and safely by matching circuit amperage to a table of appropriate wire sizes. The values on the AC table below are based on the NEC (National Electrical Code) ratings for household systems (which shore-power systems imitate).

AWG WIRE GAUGE	MAXIMUM CURRENT
#16	10A
#14	15A
#12	20A
#10	30A
#8	40A
#6	55A

Figure 13-2

Working on electrical systems should not be undertaken lightly. Do not attempt it if some aspect is unclear to you. Do not inspect or work on any electrical system that has not been disconnected from its power source. Any discussion of more extensive, high-power systems has been purposely omitted from this chapter in the strong belief that such systems and their increased complexity and potential for hazards should be left in the hands of professionals who have the experience and specialized tools to do the job properly.

Chapter Fourteen
Future Lights

I go through the same routine every spring. As soon as the tarp is off the boat, I make the rounds to every light on board, remove the lens, scrub any corrosion off the bulb's contacts and its receptacle, test it, maybe replace it, then move on to the next. It's a tedious task, but when you have electrical contacts, often of dissimilar metals, in a humid or even salty environment, you have to deal with corrosion. The alternative is risking that you'll find yourself without lights when you need them most.

Of all of the inventions that make modern boating what it is, only a few are older than the lightbulb. Batteries were invented more than 200 years ago. Propellers came 50 years later. The incandescent bulb was patented in 1897 by Thomas Edison, and its basic form and operation have changed surprisingly little in the 100 years since. In spite of the invention of other ways to generate light such as fluorescent, arc and various halide lamps, the incandescent bulb still provides a great majority of the light in use today. But that's changing rapidly, and the change bodes well for boaters.

The agent for change is the light-emitting diode or LED. LEDs are tiny devices encapsulated in clear plastic that emit light when a small current of electricity is passed through them. Their plastic bodies can be shaped into lenses which focus their output fairly accurately. The smallest ones are the size of a sesame seed; the largest are about peanut-size. Early ones produced only a faint glow, but the more recent development of higher-intensity LEDs has opened up many new uses for them. The color depends on the materials used in the diodes' manufacturing process. Red, green and yellow diodes are easy to make and are therefore quite common. Researchers have been working hard to develop bright diodes in other colors, especially blue, because a combination of red, green and blue emitted simultaneously will result in the long-sought-after white LED.

There are many reasons to use LEDs, but the primary attractions are their efficiency and very long life. An incandescent lamp makes light by passing a strong electric current through a filament of tungsten wire which, because of its resistance to the current, gets white-hot and gives off light. However, most of the electricity it consumes isn't converted to visible light but wasted in the creation of heat and infrared radiation, neither of which is useful in a light source. In addition to being very fragile, the filament has a finite life, so the lamp has to be replaced periodically.

The power consumed by an LED, however, is used much more efficiently, creating more light than heat, so it's not self-destructive. And since it's a solid-state device and has all of its parts encased in solid plastic, it's extremely rugged. These features add up to provide a useful life that can stretch to a million hours or more, so that most LEDs are permanently soldered in place. They are lifetime components that are rapidly finding their way into everyday use. Those bright new traffic lights that look like a field of glowing dots are made up of hundreds of LEDs, as are those directional lights on trucks that startle you with their strobe-like flashes. The brake-light bars on many cars are another growing use. Taillights are next.

When and how will all these benefits trickle down to boaters? Soon. It takes a while for new technology to reach us. Electronic ignition systems were available in cars for years while boaters were still struggling with points and condensers in their ignition distributors. LEDs won't be far behind.

High-intensity red and green LEDs have been available for several years, but their prices are only now starting to come down. White LEDs were not available at all, but at least three manufacturers, including Germany's Siemens, will soon have production up and running.

LED navigation lights will bring several important benefits to boaters. Their long life means never having to worry about replacing bulbs again, and there will be no sockets or pins or connections to corrode and fail. They'll be permanently soldered in place, and all of their wiring will be encapsulated in plastic or a conformal coating to permanently protect it from the elements.

Other uses will soon follow. For chart tables and interior lighting, red LED light is the perfect color to protect your vision while running at night. White LEDs are already being designed into automotive interior and courtesy lights, which means that efficient interior lighting for marine use is a future possibility. Their stingy use of electricity will reduce your need to follow the family around to shut off lights to protect your batteries.

An even wider application of LEDs will be their use on aids to navigation, where their long life will dramatically reduce maintenance cost, and their reduced appetite for power will permit the use of smaller, less expensive solar cells and batteries. A cylindrical array of 128 LEDs operating at full brightness, for example,

Modern Boatworks -- By David S. Yetman

would consume less than eight watts, about the equivalent of two household night lights.

For all their benefits, LEDs have one temporary drawback: cost. A single high-intensity LED can cost as much as $3. Most are closer to $1 and falling, but because of their tiny size and relatively modest output, they must be used in arrays in applications such as navigation or interior lights. That means that a single navigation light for a small craft might have 30 or more LEDs in order to attain the needed brightness and coverage. Their cost and the cost of assembling them results in a high initial price. True, it will be repaid many times over by the lack of maintenance and replacement, but that doesn't compensate for that hurdle.

Because of the initial cost disadvantage, we can expect to see LED lights to appear in the high end of the boat market first. Buyers of expensive boats will demand the latest and greatest, and the price will easily hide the extra cost of high-tech lights. Then the prices will begin to fall, and like radar, loran and GPS before them, they'll soon start showing up on boats for the rest of us. Until then, I've resigned myself to doing what I have to in the spring.

Chapter Fifteen
Communications Afloat

Modern mariners rely upon few things more heavily than their electronic systems. That reliance is so entrenched that traditionalists worry that fewer and fewer of us can safely navigate a passage with nothing but a compass, sextant and chronometer, but that's a fact of modern life.

It's also true that recreational boating as we know it simply would not exist, had the electronics not become available. Fortunately, advances in science over the past few years have made reliable, solid-state electronics available to everyone, even those with a modest budget. But in spite of their sophistication and apparent diversity, most marine electronics still share a reliance on a technology that's been around for more than a century.

With the exception of compasses and sonar-based underwater devices, marine electronics rely on some form of communication. VHF, loran, radar, satcom, SSB (single sideband) and even GPS systems depend upon signals that are broadcast via electromagnetic waves at various frequencies. For simplicity's sake, we'll call them radio waves. Our ability to communicate by radio, whether it's person-to-person or satellite-to-receiver, is directly affected by many environmental conditions, including terrestrial weather, local interference, position, distance, and most of all the sun, which controls the weather in space.

In addition to the energy we can see and feel, the sun produces prodigious amounts of ultra-violet (UV) and X-ray radiation, which cause temporary changes in the gases that make up our atmosphere, specifically in the ionosphere, a multi-layer band between 30 and 260 miles above the earth's surface.

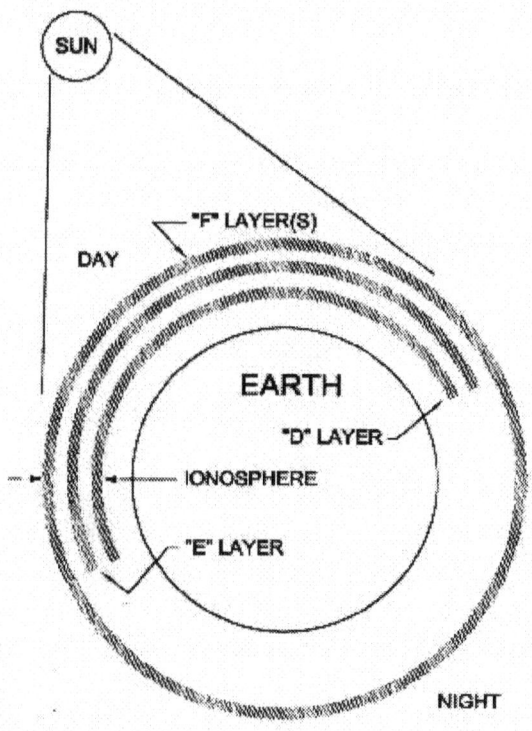

Figure 15-1

The difference in ionispheric layers during the day and at night.

The ionosphere is made up of several fairly distinct layers of gases, mainly oxygen and nitrogen, with lesser amounts of hydrogen, helium and ozone. In the discussion of their role in radio communications, however, only the D, E and F layers are relevant. (See Figure 1.) These layers vary in their makeup and density in relationship to their distance from the earth's surface. They also exhibit different characteristics based on their exposure (or lack of it, at night) to UV and X-ray energy from the sun. When the atoms of gas absorb the sun's radiation, they lose an electron, becoming positively charged ions in the process known as ionization. The increased level of ionization in the layers alters their effect on radio waves, but in different ways from layer to layer.

  The D layer, at an altitude of 30 to 55 miles, is closest to the earth's surface and therefore the most dense. When it becomes ionized, it tends to allow radio waves to pass through rather than reflect them, but it absorbs some of their energy as they pass through. By contrast, the E layer, at an altitude between 60 and 70 miles, becomes more reflective with ionization. Both D and E rapidly lose their ionization when denied sunlight by the earth's shadow and thus "disappear" at night.

  The F layer, from 100 to 260 miles, is actually two sub-layers that combine at night to form a single high-altitude layer that loses its ionization very slowly, remaining an excellent reflector for sky waves and providing enhanced long-distance communication throughout the evening hours for users of the high-frequency bands up to 30 MHz and occasionally higher. The F layer is the primary reflector of high-frequency radio waves.

  From a communication perspective, the D layer is the one to watch. Under normal conditions, the effects of its ionization are only seen as the difference between daytime communication, when the D layer exists, and the usually longer distance obtainable during communication at night, when it disappears. The phenomenon has been studied extensively, and its effects are well documented, but how it affects on radio communication depends on what frequency is being used.

Radio signals are produced by transmitters and carried by electromagnetic waves of different lengths and forms (depending on frequency), which propagate to distant receivers. In high-frequency transmission, below about 30 megahertz (MHz), they take the form of sky waves. Communication in the very high frequency (VHF) range (140mHz) and above, is via direct waves. At very low frequencies, ground waves are generated. All are shown in Figure 2.

Sky waves travel upward at an angle from the transmitting antenna and are reflected back by the ionosphere, covering great distances in the process (1,200 to 2,500 miles are not uncommon). (See Figure 2.) During daylight hours, however, the lowest layer of the ionosphere becomes ionized, so it absorbs varying amounts of the signal rather than bounce it back. This lower layer subjects sky waves to double jeopardy because they must pass through once on the way up and again on the way down after being reflected by the layers above.

Direct waves result in what we normally call line-of-sight communication, which is usually limited to about 20 miles under average conditions. With the exception of loran and SSB, most marine electronics operate at frequencies above 140 MHz, so they use direct waves and don't rely on ionospheric bounce for the signal to reach the intended receivers.

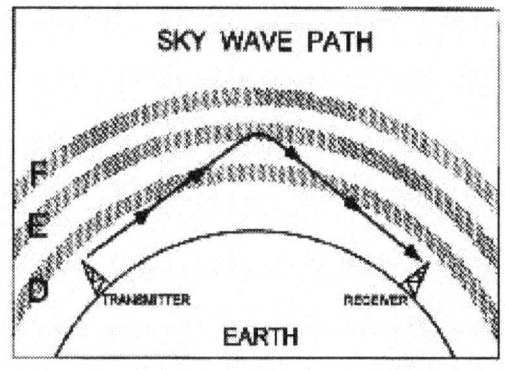
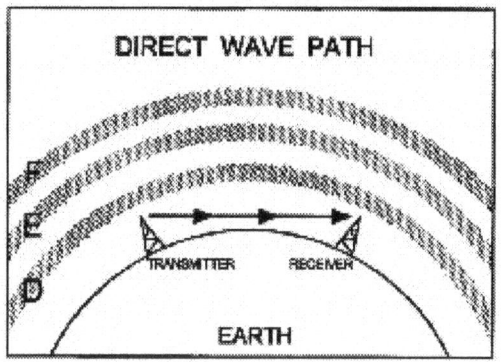
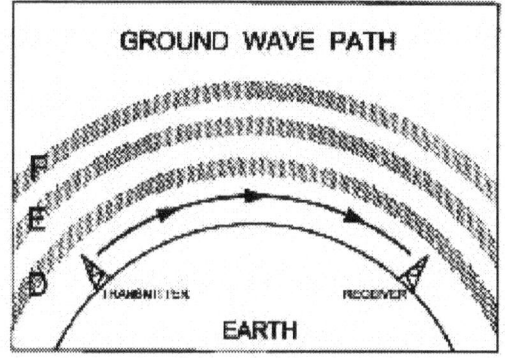

Figure 15-2

Comparative paths of radio waves.

Ground waves, as their name implies, travel along the earth's surface and permit signals to be transmitted over very long distances. Loran, which operates at 100 kHz, relies on ground waves. Like direct waves, their principal mode of propagation doesn't rely on ionospheric bounce.

But what about the GPS system, with its constellation of satellites spinning 11,000 nautical miles above the ionosphere? It differs from other marine communication systems in that the transmitter is in the satellite above the ionosphere and the receiver is below it. Thus, the communication between them must pass through all the layers of the ionosphere.

GPS isn't immune to the influence of the weather in space. Tony Adams, a senior research engineer for Raytheon in Portsmouth, England, has information indicating that, in the absence of any correction, the daylight margin of positional error due to the effects of ionization can be 10 times greater than it is at night.

Fortunately, the GPS system has several attributes that minimize this effect. First, the satellites transmit their information at extremely high frequencies, where radio waves are not as susceptible to attenuation by the ionosphere as they would be at lower frequencies. Second, and more importantly, the receivers have the capability to include an ionospheric correction factor into their computation of position. This factor is based on a model of the ionosphere which is continuously updated by the system and periodically downloaded to the receivers. This allows them to adjust to evolving conditions such as the cyclical increase in ionization. Positional errors are a possible result, but they will be insignificant compared to the deliberate error factor that the Department of Defense formerly inflicted via selective availability.

Marine electronics serve us very well. They will continue to become more reliable and useful as their technology is merged with computers and their ability to communicate is expanded to the Internet. You may not be able to surf the Net with your GPS, but you'll be able to take comfort in the fact that it has downloaded the latest software fix from its manufacturer and received the latest satellite condition information from NOAA, all while you were busy pulling that fish over the transom.

Note: Weather in space, radio communication and marine electronics are complex subjects, each a science in its own right. A wealth of information is available for those who choose to delve more deeply. Two particularly rich sources are IPS Radio and Space Services, a service of the Australian government (http://www.ips.gov.au) for information on weather in space, and the many publications of the American Radio Relay League (http://www.arrl.org) for radio communication and wave propagation information. Other sources are the Goddard Space Flight Center's High Energy Solar Imager homepage (http://hesperia.gsfc.nasa.gov) and the U.S. Naval Observatory (http://www.usno.navy.mil).

SOLAR FLARES & MARINE COMMUNICATION

Even the most sophisticated electronics are at the mercy of the unpredictable natural weather environment, and nature has an inexhaustible basket of tricks to choose from.

None is capable of more dramatic disruption than solar flares. Solar flares are huge outbursts at the sun's surface, which release energy at many wavelengths in the radio, visible, ultra-violet and X-ray bands of the electromagnetic spectrum. They are the result of interaction between different magnetic fields on the sun as it rotates.

Under the right combination of conditions, the resulting build-up of energy can be released in an explosive event, a solar flare. In addition to the burst of electromagnetic radiation, they can also be accompanied by the release of clouds of charged particles that can reach the earth in the form of a geomagnetic storm. The quantity of energy released in a single solar flare can be equivalent to more than a million hydrogen bombs, and temperatures within the event can reach tens of millions of degrees. Even though the flare's energy is scattered throughout the solar system, enough reaches the earth to cause changes in the ionosphere.

These flares occur all the time but greatly increase in frequency in a nine- to-11 year cycle. The episode of the late 1980s is being followed by another period of increased activity in 2001 and again around 2011.

Most radio communication is affected one way or the other by levels of ionization in the atmosphere, and these levels go up dramatically in response to increased solar flare activity. Increased amounts of X-ray radiation cause at least one layer of the ionosphere to become highly absorbent of radio waves. The result can be strong enough to severely disrupt or even prevent communication entirely for periods known as shortwave fade-outs. Disruption reaches its peak in a matter of minutes, but it may take one hour or several hours for communications at the affected frequencies to return to normal. The only marine communication normally subject to this severe disruption is SSB.

The other phenomenon associated with solar flares, such as noise and static, may affect VHF communication. It is not subject to the extreme disruption that may affect other forms of communication that rely on sky waves.

The effect of ionization on GPS can affect its accuracy, which implies that the margin of error would be even greater during times of increased solar activity. The system's ability to adjust its calculations allows it to compensate for night-to-day and seasonal fluctuations but not to very rapid changes such as a burst of ionization caused by a solar flare. These will cause a temporary degradation of accuracy.

All marine radio communication is susceptible to the effects of solar weather on the ionosphere. Prudent mariners will remain aware of the potential for disruption and, as always, not rely on a single device or system for navigation and communication.

Modern Boatworks -- By David S. Yetman

Chapter Sixteen
Antenna Basics

It wasn't too long ago that you had to have a fair amount of technical knowledge to operate marine electronics. A quick look at a 30-year-old VHF or loran receiver will be a revelation if you've never seen one before. Thankfully, the latest gear has come a long way in quality, convenience and affordability, so that even the least technically competent among us can now use a VHF transceiver or GPS without saddling ourselves with an in-depth understanding of its esoterica.

That's the good news. The bad news is that our arm's-length relationship with technology can lead us to use it in a manner that defeats some of its benefits. Antennas are a good example.

VHF antennas have a smooth, uncluttered exterior that masks the complex make-up of precisely designed internal elements, but they are among the most highly engineered equipment available to boaters. There are a bewildering number of them on the market, separated mainly by differences in the quality of design and construction, but from a performance standpoint there are three separate types to choose from, differentiated by a factor called gain.

Gain is the ability of an antenna to focus its output into a narrow band perpendicular to its axis and is expressed in units called decibels (dB). Marine VHF antennas are commonly available in 3, 6 and 9dB ratings.

As shown in Figure 1, the higher the antenna's gain, the more focused its output will be. (Figure 1 doesn't represent actual patterns but is meant to show the relative difference in output.)

At first glance, it would seem that the greatest benefit would come from using a 9dB antenna, concentrating the signal as much as possible toward the intended receiver. That would be true if boats were highly stable platforms, but except for very large vessels, this isn't the case. The antenna's output is directed up or down, away from the intended target as the boat rolls and pitches, causing the signal to fade in and out. In addition, most 9dB antennas are about 20 feet long and must be firmly supported at several points, making them impractical on small boats. Most examples of this type have a sealed fiberglass or urethane outer sheath to protect their copper or brass internal components and require little maintenance other than cleaning.

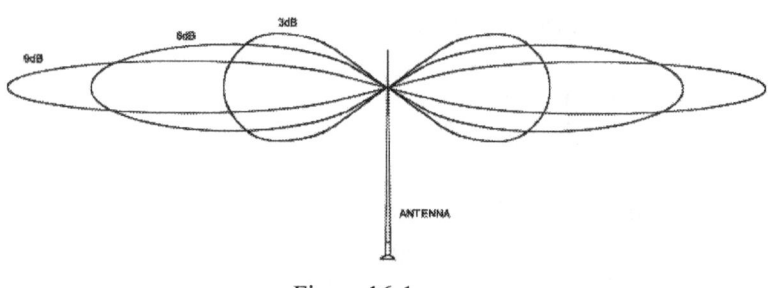

Figure 16-1

Comparative output waveforms of antennas.

At the other end of the spectrum, a 3dB antenna provides the greatest signal spread but at a cost of less effectiveness at greater distances. They are most often used on sailboats because their performance will suffer less when the boat is heeled over and can be mounted high on the mast to help overcome their reduced efficiency. Their small size and performance also make them practical on very small boats. Most antennas of this type are comprised of a stainless-steel whip mounted on a small canister that encloses a "base-loading" coil.

The most common VHF marine antenna by far is the 6dB gain, eight-foot type. Most offer reliable boat-to-boat communications over a 10- to 15-mile range when properly installed and mounted as high as possible. Communication with a shore-based facility whose antenna is even higher may be possible beyond that range. The 6dB antenna provides the best balance between manageable size, ease of mounting and performance, which is more than adequate for most near-shore applications. However, its performance and efficiency are easily defeated.

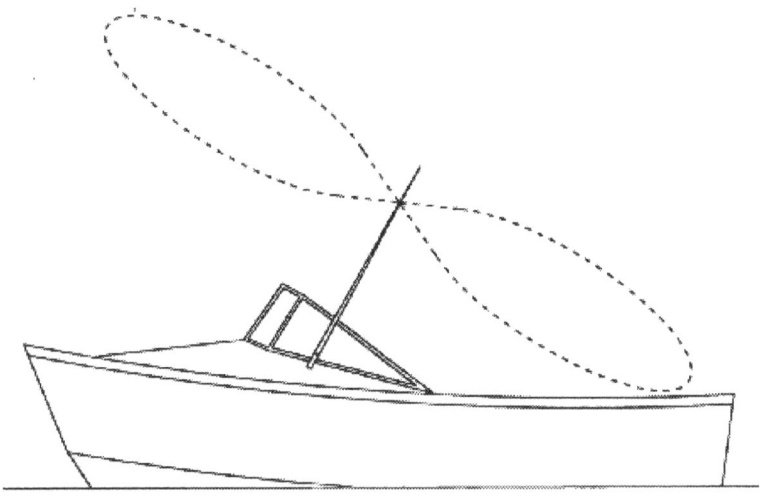

Figure 16-2

Misdirected output resulting from a tilted antenna..

Modern Boatworks -- *By David S. Yetman*

Figure 2 shows an extreme but common example of improper positioning. The boat's owner has chosen to mount the antenna at a rakish angle to match the slant of his windshield at the expense of communication with stations forward or aft of his position. He may only notice occasional problems when cruising along the shore, but long-distance communication in an emergency could suffer significantly. Another version of the same problem can crop up in radar installations where the radome is mounted in a level position with the boat at rest, only to have its operation compromised when the boat assumes a bow-up position while under way and the radar views nothing but sky.

Mounting an antenna on your boat is a task that can be done quickly or well. A top-notch job requires some planning and may take a little longer, it but will result in a better looking, better performing installation. Modern boats offer very few truly horizontal, vertical or flat places to mount an antenna, so some ingenuity on your part may be required. Even if you choose a fancy adjustable mount such as shown in Figure 3, you'll find their toothed adjustments are coarse ones that don't always adjust to the exact angle you'd like. The example in Figure 3 is mounted to the sloping side of a cuddy cabin, requiring the use of shim washers behind the top mounting screws to bring the mount to a vertical position. The resulting gap behind the bracket can be filled with marine sealant and finished off with a neat fillet around the outside.

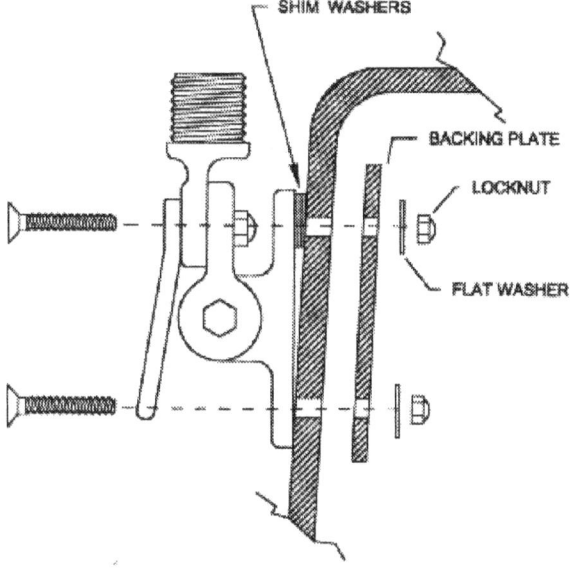

Figure 16-3

Correct installation of an antenna mount.

Whip antennas take quite a beating on a boat, especially one used offshore in rough water. The constant bouncing and pounding can loosen up mounting hardware in a hurry, so it's important to use the proper type. Most commercially available mounts will allow you to use 1/4 inch screws. These should be inserted through clearance holes in the boat's panel, through a metal backing plate and secured with elastic stop nuts. Ordinary lock washers depend on being very tightly compressed, whereas nylon lock-nuts will hold tenaciously without being over tightened. The difference is important when the screw is going through wood or plastic, which can compress under a load. (If a metal backing plate is impractical, use large diameter fender washers instead.)

Modern Boatworks -- By David S. Yetman

    The efficiency of VHF antennas and whip antennas in general can also be profoundly affected by the proximity of other metallic objects, especially parallel ones of similar shape. Keeping antennas safely separated not only ensures their efficient operation but protects other sensitive instruments such as GPS receivers from having their amplifiers fried by a blast of 25-watt transmitter power from your VHF.

    Communication and navigation technologies continue to advance by leaps and bounds. For those who don't have the time or inclination to immerse ourselves in the technical details, the best way to reap their maximum benefit is to carefully install and maintain the equipment according to the manufacturers' instructions. Having done that, you'll be able to devote more time to important stuff like keeping the bait alive and the drinks cold.

Chapter Seventeen
VHF at Home

Like many avid boaters, my interest in what's happening on the water doesn't shut down when I go ashore, so I always keep a hand-held VHF on a shelf in the kitchen. But once the newness wore off, the constant recharging, uneven reception and poor sound quality made it seem a less-than-ideal way of staying in touch. What I really needed was a receiver that ran on house power with a reasonably large speaker and a more efficient antenna. There didn't seem to be a system that fit that description on the market, so I put one together myself.

While the thought of building a VHF may seem daunting, it's a project that can be undertaken at different levels. At its most simplistic level, it consists of tying together some purchased parts and requires very little expertise. At the other end of the spectrum, you can get carried away with custom cabinets and more demanding electronics.

A bare-bones system can be nothing more than a VHF receiver, a power supply to convert household AC to 12-volt DC and an antenna. If a more finished look or better sound is important, the system can be scaled up with the addition of a larger speaker for better sound and an enclosure for the receiver

Antenna

Important considerations in selecting an antenna are things like the distance from your home to the activity you want to monitor, the probable location of the antenna on or within your home, and how you intend to use the system. Keep in mind that in most situations, VHF communication is "line-of-sight," so the highest mounting point you can find will be the most satisfactory. The best choice may be the standard eight-foot whip on your roof or in your attic. A 34-inch mast-top or flatboat antenna is the next best and also easier to find space for. They cost less, are easier to handle and are compact enough so that they can even be mounted on the back of a bookcase or in a closet. Even simpler, a single wire attached to the center terminal of the antenna connector will suffice for receiving-only or strictly local operation in some instances. Performance of any antenna will be affected by the proximity of metal objects such as window screens, plumbing or other wiring, so choose an acceptable location before permanently mounting the antenna.

Receiver

Most VHF receivers offer similar sets of performance features, but make sure the one you choose has a jack for an extension speaker if improved sound is part of your plan. The ability to scan multiple channels is a real convenience for unattended operation as well. Beyond that and personal preferences, the other consideration is receiver sensitivity; good units are more sensitive and better able to lock onto weak signals. Look for a rating of 0.25lV to 0.30lV or better. The lower the number, the more sensitive the receiver will be.

From a mechanical standpoint, features like an available or built-in flange (as opposed to just a rectangular case) will make mounting the unit in an enclosure a much easier job.

Power Supply

VHF transceivers for marine use run on 12-V DC, so a power supply that converts 110-V AC to 12-V DC is a necessity in order to use it ashore. The power supply is technically the opposite of an inverter. The primary consideration in choosing a power supply is its output capacity specified in watts or amps. For stand-by operation only, the average transceiver will draw only 0.5 amps (6 watts). When receiving, this will increase to 1.5 amps (18 watts). To transmit on low (1 watt output), the draw will be more like 2 or 3 amps (24-36 watts). Transmitting on high (25 watts output) will require around 6 amps (72 watts). The output power of the transmitter will always be considerably less than the input power because of natural inefficiencies and the power it takes to run the unit itself. Using a power supply whose output capabilities are lower than the transmitter's requirement will overload the supply and limit the strength of the output signal. Continuous or severe overloading of the power supply may result in eventual failure of the supply. (Keep in mind that it is illegal to use a VHF marine radio to transmit from a shore location unless you have an FCC license to do so. The elimination of license requirements for recreational boaters did not eliminate the need to have one for shore-based transmission.)

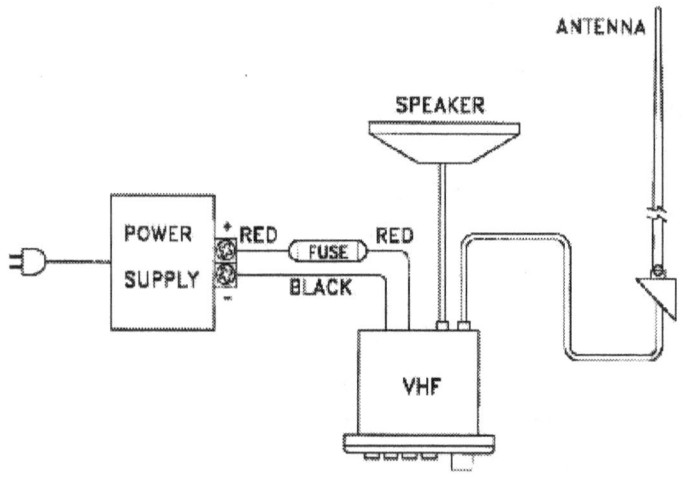

Figure 17-1

Wiring diagram of an AC-powered VHF radio.

Power supplies are available in many marine, hobby and electronics stores as well as from mail-order sources. Though they are nominally rated at 12 volts, many will actually put out up to 14 volts or so, but this is well within the operating range of most marine equipment. Most general-purpose power supplies are sold as enclosed units. The enclosed type are much easier to use, safer and more convenient for the casual user because their inputs and outputs are clearly defined, mounting points are provided and they require no special electrical knowledge. Those sold without enclosures are called open-frame supplies and are meant to be included in other equipment which will provide the safety of an enclosure. They also demand more involvement from the user, since their terminals may not be clearly marked, and they often require special input and output connectors. Using an open-frame supply can also put you in violation of local electrical codes if done inappropriately. The best and safest bet is an enclosed supply. The electrical hook-up is shown in Figure 1.

Building the System

There are as many ways to do this as there are people who want to do it. Some will settle for nothing less than a custom cabinet, and the ambitious system shown here is an example of that. It has an oak-trimmed Formica-covered cabinet and a 3" speaker and a power switch on its front panel. In addition to woodworking skills, the builder had some electrical experience, so chose to use a compact open-frame power supply.

An easier, simpler alternative is to install the components into an existing speaker enclosure. Inexpensive extension speakers are available in electronics outlets or can be salvaged from a discarded tabletop stereo system. If two speakers are available, consider putting the electronics in one and using the other as a remote. An opening for the receiver can be cut in the front panel of the cabinet with a sabre saw or a keyhole saw. (Remove the speaker and put it safely aside while the work is in process.) If the grille cloth isn't adhered to the front panel, apply a thin line of glue just outside of the intended opening and let it cure before making the cut. This will prevent the cloth from unraveling when you cut through it. The power supply can be mounted in the opposite end of the enclosure. If it has an off/on switch, make sure you position the supply so that the switch is accessible. Otherwise, a UL-approved in-line switch (available at hardware stores) can be inserted into the power supply's line cord. More often than not, the speaker will already be equipped with an RCA-type audio plug that will connect right into the receiver's extension-speaker outlet. The speaker's rear cover should be well ventilated or removed entirely to provide cooling for the VHF and power supply, both of which generate a considerable amount of heat during operation.

Figure 17-2
A VHF radio mounted in a custom cabinet.

Figure 17-3
Bottom view of the cabinet showing the location of its components.

Figure 17-4

A VHF radio mounted in a speaker enclosure for home use.

nce the components are connected together, you only have to plug in the antenna to be back in touch with the good life on the water.

Figure 17-5

The 12-volt power supply is mounted above the speaker in this rear view.

Chapter Eighteen
Surviving An Electrical Disaster

The script is familiar because we've all thought about the possibility at one time or another.

It's a beautiful afternoon, you're anchored at your favorite fishing spot and the big ones are biting. The shoreline is just a smudge on the horizon, but the sea is calm and the wind is only a warm zephyr.

Then it changes. The gentle southwesterly freshens and backs around to the southeast, then east, and the temperature drops a degree or two. In no time at all the weather will be from the northeast, and you know this is no place for a 22-footer with four people on board.

"Time to go", you announce. "Reel 'em in and stow your gear. We're outta here."

After emptying the baitwells, you move the coolers forward and assign stations to everyone; there's nothing worse than a heavy stern in a following sea. Then you switch on the bilge blower and make a final check of the cockpit. Satisfied that everything's in shape, you turn the ignition key and are rewarded with silence. You notice the bilge blower isn't making any noise either, and there's no light behind the dial of your VHF. Your four-year-old battery has let you down with a thud.

Modern Boatworks -- By David S. Yetman

With the VHF dead, you can't call a tow, but the third try at *CG on your cell phone puts you in touch with the Coast Guard. They want to know your exact location, but your GPS is out too. Daylight and the cell phone's battery are fading fast, but your luck holds out. A sail appears on the horizon and changes course in your direction after you've fired your next-to-last flare.

With the exception of a holed hull, few boating situations can match a total electrical failure for creating a sense of helplessness and danger. Nearly every system on modern boats, from starting to communication, relies on electrical power. Systems have improved dramatically with the advent of solid-state ignition and electronic engine control, but their foundation is still an ancient invention called the storage battery, which has changed very little in the last 200 years. Marine electrical systems require vigilance, maintenance and occasional updating to remain reliable.

Murphy's Law applies at sea as it does on land, but you can do a number of things that will help you avoid extreme consequences when it catches up with your electrical system.

The marine environment (moisture, corrosion and vibration) is harsh for electrical devices, and without constant maintenance they will suffer. But vigilance is important too. Vigilance consists of being aware of the state of the system. How are things running? How old is the battery? When did you last check its connections or fluid level? What has given you trouble previously and deserves an occasional look? What's the condition of your spare bulbs and fuses?

Maintenance and vigilance will be more effective if you have some knowledge of electricity. You don't need an electrical engineering degree, but a basic understanding of continuity and the relationship between voltage, current and resistance (Ohm's Law) will help.

After you've done everything you can to prevent them, the final line of defense against electrical emergencies is to be prepared.

Be prepared to search out the problem, fix it if you can, and if all else fails, rely on a backup source of power to allow you to call for assistance and operate navigation aids.

You need an electrical emergency kit. Being well prepared is like buying insurance — as long as you don't use it, it looks like a waste of money, but you can put an electrical emergency kit together quickly and inexpensively. Once you've assembled it, the kit can be stowed out of the way and will require only a seasonal check-up. Assuming that you already have screwdrivers, pliers and a sharp knife in your regular tool kit, the electrical one should contain at a minimum:

1. An inexpensive electrical tester (Volt/Ohm meter) such as Radio Shack's model 22-218 (under $20).

2. A pair of six-foot 14-gauge wires with color-coded alligator clips on the ends (black on one, red on the other).

3. A second pair of wires with alligator clips on one end and banana plugs on the other.

4. A selection of spare fuses whose values match those used in equipment on your boat.

5. A selection of spare bulbs to match those used on board.

6. Twelve-volt power adapters and spare alkaline batteries for any hand-held electronics you carry.

7. A pair of diagonal wire-cutting pliers.

8. A roll of electrical tape.

9. A small, moisture-resistant flashlight equipped with alkaline batteries.

10. A small mirror.

11. Safety pins.

12. A back-up power source.

The Backup Power Source

This can be as minimal as a pair of six-volt lantern batteries connected in series to produce 12 volts. Spend the extra money for alkaline batteries. Their shelf life and storage capacity make them the only choice for stand-by emergency power. They should be wired up as shown in Figure 1, with #16 (or larger) connecting wires soldered to their terminals. The quickest and most convenient way to access their power is through connectors wired to them. A cigarette-lighter receptacle is useful for connecting a hand-held GPS or cell phone if yours are so equipped. A pair of multi-purpose terminals (like Radio Shack # 274-661, about $1 each) have receptacles for banana plugs and will also act as screw-down binding posts for the connection of bare wires. Remember that positive (+) connections are usually made with red connectors or wires, and ground or negative (-) connections to black ones. Wrap all bare connections generously with insulating electrical tape to prevent them from shorting out.

The lantern-battery set will not provide enough power to operate a built-in VHF in the high (25 watt) range; it takes more current than the batteries will produce. But it will power a VHF in the low (1-watt) range for several hours. It will also run a GPS, a hand-held cell phone or hand-held VHF, which draw less than 1 amp while transmitting.

A second option is a jump-starting kit such as Prestone's "Jump-It," which has more than enough power to operate a VHF at 25 watts. Although they cost more (about $100), they are unquestionably a better choice for offshore cruisers. They have the added advantage of being self-contained, portable and, according to the manufacturer, able to jump-start your engine as well.

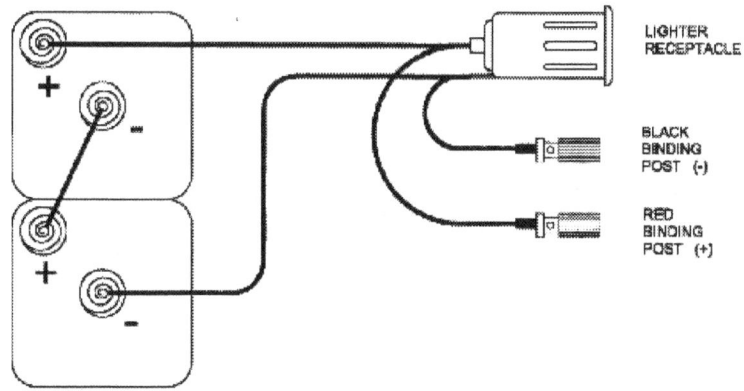

Figure 18-1
Wiring diagram for an emergency 12-volt power source.

Using the Kit

There are as many uses for the kit as there are problems, but we'll look at some of the most useful. Most VOM testers in this price range will have two or three functions. They will measure AC and DC voltage, usually in several ranges. They will measure resistance in ohms, also in several ranges. Many may also have the ability to measure current, but the amount of current will probably be in the milliampere (1/1000 of an ampere) range, making them all but useless for marine systems. These typically draw much more than that.

Modern Boatworks -- By David S. Yetman

Figure 18-2
Contents of a basic electrical emergency kit.

The DC voltage function is useful primarily for finding what's live and what's not in the boat's basic 12-volt electrical system. It's operated by touching or attaching its black test lead to ground and its red lead to a terminal or wire that's supposed to be live. The voltage (if any) will be shown on the meter. If the meter's needle tries to move backwards, you have the leads reversed. If you need to check out the status of a wire where there are no open terminals, you can stick a safety pin through the insulation into the wire and attach the test lead to the pin. (Wrap some electrical tape around the pinhole when you're through to keep moisture out.)

If your boat has a shore-power system or a 110-volt generator, be sure to disconnect or shut it down before inspecting unknown circuits or wiring.

DC voltage is also useful for judging the quality of a supply line or connection. Attach its leads to a device such as a pump, with the pump and your engine off. The meter should read around 12 volts. If the voltage drops more than 10 percent or so when you turn on the device, you may have an inadequate connection. The greater the drop, the more serious the situation may be. The problem could be a frayed or corroded wire or a wire size too small for its load.

Resistance function is most useful in emergency situations when used as a continuity tester to see if two points or terminals are electrically connected to each other. Use the lowest resistance range and touch the test leads to the two points you want to evaluate. If there's a good connection between them, the meter will move nearly to its maximum. To prevent damage to the meter, check for the presence of voltage in the circuit you're trying to inspect before you check for continuity using the resistance function. If you find a voltage present, switch the circuit off if possible, or switch off or disconnect the battery.

The mirror and the small flashlight will come in handy for inspecting out-of-the-way connections. The sets of wires with clips attached can be used to extend the meter leads where necessary, or to temporarily bypass a faulty switch or broken wire. They can also be used to deliver power to a device that's not getting any. For example, if you need to use a radio when your battery's dead, disconnect it from the system by removing its fuse before attaching it to your emergency power source so the dead battery (or short circuit) won't drain off the power from the source.

Whatever you choose as a back-up power source, remember that it will need maintenance. A jump-start kit will require occasional charging. Unused alkaline batteries will last several years, usually well after their "use by" date, but because they're part of your safety gear, you should replace the batteries with new ones after two or three years. The old ones may still give good service in a lantern-type flashlight, so don't recycle them immediately. And don't forget to replace the batteries in the VOM and the flashlight while you're at it.

If all of this sounds like more insurance than you want, at least include some of the components in your tool kit, especially if yours is an older boat. The tester, fuses, tape and jumper wires can be important. A couple of lantern batteries taped together and stowed in a plastic bag somewhere could save your boat and your life. Someone once said survival is 10 percent luck and 90 percent hard work. I'd say the split is more like 50-50 between work and being well-prepared.

Modern Boatworks -- By David S. Yetman

Chapter Nineteen
CAD for Your Projects

I'm an inveterate tinkerer. Leaving well-enough alone is failure to rise to a challenge as far as I'm concerned. In my younger days, I wouldn't be seen in a car that hadn't been customized. When I graduated to sports cars, I dismayed the purists by modifying them, too. When I moved on to motorcycles, the only time I ever rode a stocker was bringing it home from the dealership. Even my first entrepreneurial fling was based on change, manufacturing conversion kits for cyclists like me who wanted to turn their bikes into café racers.

It would be unreasonable to expect me to abandon my ways just because I discovered boats.

Driving back from the dealership where I'd just ordered my first boat, I thought about the changes I'd have to make when it arrived. It would need a new instrument panel to accommodate the flush-mount VHF and Loran. I'd have to install an opening hatch in the cuddy cabin. The canvas top would have to be modified to be used as a bimini. On and on it went. It was November, nearly six months before she'd be delivered, so there was ample time for the list to grow.

I spent much of that winter shuttling back and forth between the dealer's showroom and my home office. The dealer had a display model of my boat that I could inspect, measure, trace and probe. My office had the computer with my computer-aided design (CAD) software on it. By the time the boat was finally delivered, I had complete plans for each of the projects, had pre-made many of the new parts and knew where every new hole and cutout would go.

In all my years as a designer and engineer, I've never had a tool that did so much for so little money as a CAD set-up. I hate to think about the thousands of hours I wasted in trial-and-error modifications before CAD came along.

Very briefly, CAD is variously used to mean computer-aided drawing, drafting or design. That's not as ambiguous as it would seem because the software will allow you to do all of those things. Some people add a D and use CADD to signify Design and Drafting, but in reality, most of the software is alike until you venture into the lofty realm of 3D design packages. CAD, the common two-dimensional variety we're discussing here, allows the user to create dimensionally accurate drawings of objects on-screen. Once created, they can be scaled up or down in size, copied or saved for re-use. Any object can be moved or copied to another location with great precision. The finished drawing will show the exact relationship between various features and allow you to show the dimensions of those relationships as well.

Even the least capable CAD software will be accurate within one thousandth of an inch, and because the software works with units rather than specific measurements, it doesn't matter whether you're using inches, feet, meters or furlongs.

You can create drawings of each object that will be on an instrument panel and move them around on a drawing of the panel itself to see where they can go, what they might interfere with and how the completed panel will look. (See Chapter 24) The resulting plans and all of their dimensions can be printed out on even the most rudimentary printers. And best of all, you don't need artistic talent to use CAD. It will create perfectly straight or parallel lines, precise arcs, circles, ellipses, squares and rectangles with a few keystrokes or mouse clicks. If you aren't familiar with the terminology of mechanical drawing or basic geometry, a few minutes with the manual will have you up-and-running in short order. Many of the packages come with a tutorial as well.

CAD really proved its value when I decided to install a pressure water system on my boat. Finding space for an electric pump, converting a baitwell to a sink and running a water line to an existing sink in the mini-galley were the easy parts. Finding a way to store a reasonable amount of fresh water was where CAD paid for itself. In doing some other work on the boat, I'd discovered about 3 cubic feet of unused space under the cockpit sole. The problem was that it was only accessible by removing some galley cabinetry, and even then you had to go around a corner to get to it. There was room for two off-the-shelf six-gallon tanks back there, but once plumbed together, they wouldn't go around the corner.

Back at the computer, I drew a rectangle that exactly represented a wooden pallet that the tanks would mount to. I drew a rectangular tank outline with its inlet, outlet and vent hole positions marked. Then I copied it so I had a pair and moved them on top of the pallet. After drawing the plumbing fittings to size, I moved them to their position on the tanks so I could determine how long each piece of connecting hose would have to be. The result was a complete top view of the two tanks and all their interconnecting hardware, which was complex because the inlets, outlets and vents had to be connected to each other and the outside world as well. Once I was satisfied that the hardware would fit the space and that the scheme was going to work, I went out and bought the parts. I built the whole rig in my shop, then took it apart and headed for the boat. There I was able to place the individual pieces in around the corner and (with a few brand-new body contortions) reconstruct the system in place. It worked — first time — and hasn't leaked a drop.

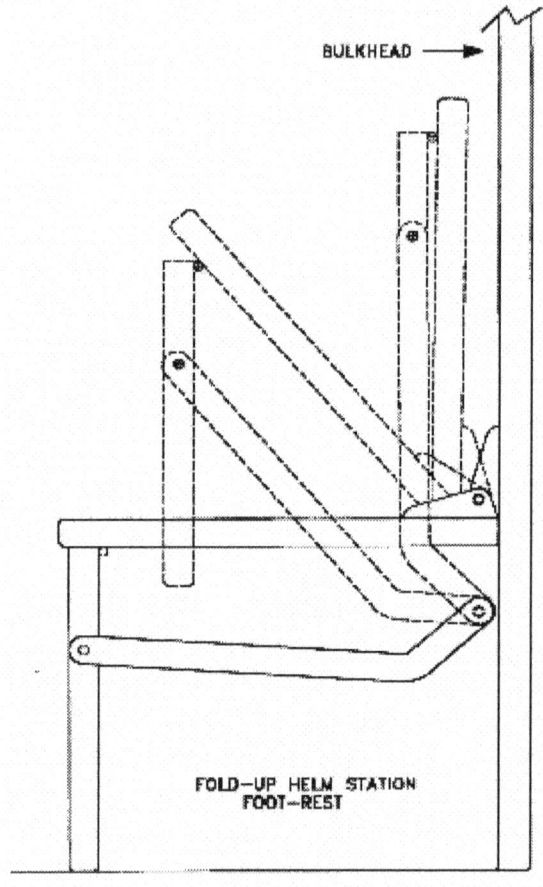

Figure 19-1

CAD-generated diagram of the action of a folding footrest.

Modern Boatworks -- By David S. Yetman

Newcomers tend to be intimidated by CAD and assume it will be both expensive and time-consuming to learn. It doesn't have to be either. While it's possible to spend more than $3,500 for industrial software like AutoCad and still have it run on a home computer, very capable software packages like AutoCad LT, AutoSketch and Generic CAD are available for $40 to $500 and will provide all of the functionality that a home- or small-business user will ever need. (Keep in mind that "street" or mail-order prices for software are usually well below list prices, so shop around.) Although I now use the latest version of AutoCad LT running under Windows (all of the illustrations in this book were drawn using it), much of my earlier work was done on AutoSketch. I have a DOS-based version I bought many years ago and have used to design everything from folding foot rests to laboratory instruments. In addition to the commercially available software, there are also shareware applications such as Draft Choice and FlashCAD for DOS and Windows that can be ordered by mail or downloaded from the Internet for a nominal charge. It's essentially free software whose authors often request only a donation from satisfied users. Shareware can be quirky and suffer incompatibility with other software packages, but in most cases these aren't issues that will bother a home user. Its other drawback is that user support, like manuals, can be scanty or non-existent. There's also a treasure trove of used CAD software available, earlier versions of DOS-based software whose status-conscious owners have moved up to the latest and greatest. If you're able to find used software, make sure you get the original diskettes and manuals in the bargain.

There are also a number of drawing (as opposed to drafting) software packages available. They tend to be rich in features such as shading and coloring but may not offer the geometric accuracy and dimensioning capabilities of true CAD, so investigate before you buy one.

Having CAD in your arsenal of tools is not just for do-it-yourselfers. It's a real asset to be able to communicate exactly what you want your radar mount to look like when you approach the craftsman who will build it. When you walk in and pull out a computer-generated drawing of what you want, you'll not only have a better chance of getting exactly what you had in mind but your credibility will rise several notches in the bargain. You're not just another guy with a sketch on the back of a beer-stained napkin.

On the other hand, if you're the craftsman, CAD will allow you to show your customer exactly what the finished work will look like, where it'll be placed and how it will affect its surroundings. The drawing can become part of the contract, eliminating much potential for misunderstanding. The short time you spend creating the drawings (which you can modify and use again and again, by the way) will be more than paid for in time saved in selling and building the goods, not to mention the benefits to your own credibility.

Whether you're an amateur, a professional or just an incorrigible tinkerer, CAD is one of the most valuable design and communication tools you can use. And if you're a traditionalist who likes to work into new things gradually, just think of it as napkins for the new millennium but without the beer stains.

Modern Boatworks -- By David S. Yetman

Chapter Twenty
Working on Fiberglass

It matters not how well-equipped she is — sooner or later you're going to want to do something to her that will require you to summon your courage, grit your teeth and put a hole in *Superscow*.

If you're like most of us, that means working with fiberglass. Whether you're just mounting another drink holder, installing electronics or carving out a hole for a hatch, there are ample opportunities for things to go wrong. Doing it right takes a little time; doing it wrong means living with the damage for a long time. Doing it right requires the right tools, a basic understanding of the material, how it's manufactured and, most of all, ways to avoid bumping into its limitations.

The term itself is a misnomer. When we say fiberglass, we're talking about fiberglass-reinforced plastic, or FRP. Real fiberglass is only the strengthening component, flexible strands of glass imbedded in a resin to give it strength. The individual strands of glass are the equivalent of steel reinforcing rods in concrete. The resin can be any number of chemical compounds which will polymerize when a catalyst is mixed into them. Polymerization is a cross-linking of molecules which, in this case, results in a liquid becoming a solid.

As the technology evolves, an increasing number of materials other than fiberglass are being used to reinforce plastics. These high-tech fibers range from boron through carbon to Kevlar, and the resulting materials are usually referred to as composites. Because of their unmatched strength-to-weight ratio, the more exotic ones are liberally used in the manufacture of tactical aircraft and control surfaces of commercial airliners, but their cost and critical manufacturing processes keep them out of the commercial realm. Some are finding their way into price-is-no-object high-performance boats, but the mainstream cruiser is still constructed of time-proven fiberglass.

Fiberglass as a commercial material owes much of its success to the persistence of General Motors after its introduction of the fiberglass-body Chevrolet Corvette in 1953. Its creators endured all of the "plastic car" jokes and sneering journalists, yet continued to insist that Corvettes, right down to the present be equipped with fiberglass bodies. In the process, their demands helped force the advance of manufacturing processes in the plastics industry, benefiting a much wider range of products (boats included).

Boat manufacturers, however, didn't exactly rush to jump on the bandwagon. Their predecessors had already suffered through the introduction of steel as a building material in the 19th century, an event that had eventually divided them into commercial- and pleasure-boat factions. They were not only being asked to abandon more than three millennia of tradition but, like their house-building brethren a century before, faced the obsolescence of their trade's lexicon as well. The new craft would need no parts called frames, knees, stems, futtocks, oakum, trunnels or knight-heads. In their place would come new terms like tensile strength, resin, catalyst, pot life, mold release compound, gel-coat, adhesives and foam cores. Boat builders would also become familiar with a whole new set of smells and develop an intimate understanding of the word "itch."

Their initial reluctance slowly diminished, though, and by the Seventies, fiberglass was the material of choice in the pleasure-boat industry.

While numerous variations are used in building custom and semi-custom boats, the majority of production fiberglass boats are assembled from molded sections. The hull, for example, is molded as a single unit complete with all of its external features including finish and color. The mold is a receptacle whose shape and internal finish will precisely determine the external appearance of the hull. In preparation for the building process, its interior surface is thoroughly cleaned before being coated with mold-release compounds (wax-like films that prevent the completed hull from sticking to the mold). Thick liquid gel-coat in the customer's choice of color is then applied to the mold's surface and allowed to cure to a specific state. This is followed by the application of successive layers of resin-soaked fiberglass until the hull is built up to its designed thickness. Stringers and other structural components are bonded in during the lay-up. Any excess is trimmed at the rim of the mold, and the resulting hull is allowed to cure before being removed. A majority of the mechanical, electrical and plumbing components will be installed in the open hull before the molded deck/cabin/cockpit structure is dropped on and attached using marine adhesives and lots of through-bolts or screws behind the rub rail.

The result is a reasonably light, strong, affordable structure that's as maintenance-free as a boat can be. However, the materials that make this possible have their limitations. Viewed from the perspective of one who wants to drill, cut or remove sections of the material, some of these limitations are:

1. Gel-coat is a notoriously brittle material. The very properties that make it so desirable as a finish (abrasion resistance and durability) require great hardness and therefore, brittleness as well. Gel-coat is very easily chipped, flaked or cracked during modifications.

2. The quality of the bond between the gel-coat and the FRP is a variable. A number of process-related factors can reduce the effectiveness of the bond. Excess gel-coat cure time, surface contamination and dry pockets in the FRP are just a few. The result is gel-coat which is easily separated from the FRP.

3. The gel-coat and FRP are dissimilar in their ability to tolerate stress. The FRP will safely absorb a level of local stress and deflection that will cause its skin of gel-coat to craze or crack.

4. The FRP can be de-laminated by improper modification. This is most often caused by screws being forced into undersize holes but can also result from other localized stresses applied to the material.

In short, fiberglass is happiest when left in its as-molded state. But if you're determined to add a cup-holder for your glass of '99 Chateau South Bronx, let's look at some less-threatening ways to perform the three most common types of fiberglass surgery: small holes for "self-tapping" screws, larger clearance holes, and finally gaping holes for things like hatches and access ports.

Small Holes for Self-Tapping Screws

Let's start with the screws; there are literally thousands of different types. One of my reference "bibles" contains nearly 300 pages of detailed information about screws, bolts, nuts and the fabrication of threads to accept them. Mercifully, only 12 different types of "self-tapping" screws exist, five of the common variety and seven which fall into the category of "thread-forming" screws. The difference is simple. Thread-forming screws have features that imitate (however crudely) a tapping die. They have cutting edges near their points which remove material in order to form internal threads for the balance of the screw to engage. Common self-tapping screws, on the other hand, are really just sheet-metal screws with no such features and rely on their ability to deform and displace material to create a path for the threads to jam into. Unfortunately, most of the stainless steel self-tapping screws available in marine stores are Type AB, which fall into the latter category. Their heavy-handed approach to getting the job done doesn't make them any less useful or reliable, but it does make them more difficult to use without causing damage to the host material.

Backing up just a bit, the best way of fastening almost anything to fiberglass is to drill clearance holes for machine screws and secure them with washers, nuts and a dab of silicone behind the bulkhead. In reality, we know that the construction of fiberglass boats rarely permits that, so we're stuck with blind holes and self-tapping hardware.

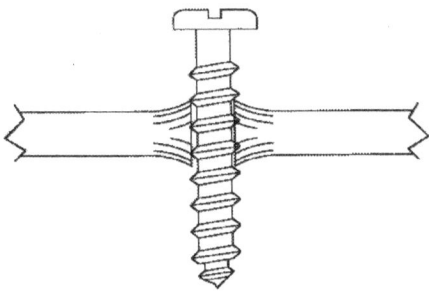

Figure 20-1
Fiberglass damage caused by improper hole sizing and preparation.

Any screw to be threaded into a fiberglass panel must be provided with a properly chamfered pilot hole of the correct diameter. The diameter of the hole is critical. A great majority of the damage inflicted when screwing into fiberglass is caused by forcing a screw into an undersize, badly prepared hole or by threading it crookedly. Figure 1 shows an exaggerated example of the results of an undersized pilot hole. The excess material is forcefully displaced by the screw, resulting in delamination of the FRP, which then blossoms up, cracking and flaking the gel-coat. The following table lists the correct diameters and corresponding drill sizes for pilot and clearance holes for standard self-tapping screw sizes up to 1/4". Please keep in mind that the pilot hole diameters are average dimensions that may have to be adjusted upwards for long screws into thick panels, or downwards for thinner panels. (See Appendix A for more information on drill sizes.)

PILOT AND CLEARANCE HOLE SIZES
Dimensions are in inches

SCREW SIZE	NOM. DIA.	PILOT HOLE DIA.	DRILL SIZE	CLEARANCE HOLE DIA.	DRILL SIZE
#4	0.112	0.101	#38	0.125	1/8
#6	0.138	0.125	1/8	0.156	5/32
#8	0.164	0.147	#26	0.188	3/16
#10	0.19	0.17	#18	0.221	7/32
#12	0.216	0.194	#10	0.025	1/4
1/4	0.25	0.228	#1	0.281	9/32

Figure 20-2

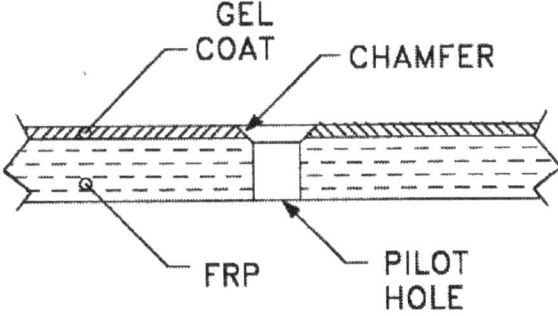

Figure 20-3
Properly prepared pilot hole for a self-tapping screw in fiberglass...

Drilling the correct size pilot hole is only the first half of the task. It is equally important to chamfer or bevel the entry to the hole so the screw threads don't come in contact with the edge of the gel-coat. Figure 3 shows a cross section of a properly chamfered pilot hole. Notice that the chamfer extends well below the gel-coat and into the FRP. Chamfering is done with a tool called a countersink, which is normally used to drill a tapered recess to accept the conical underside of the head of a flat-head screw. They're available at better hardware and industrial supply stores and are a very worthwhile addition to your tool kit. Practice using one in a scrap of hardwood or plastic before attacking *Superscow*, though.

Note: Speaking of flat-head screws, they should never be used where their head comes in contact with fiberglass. Because of their conical shape, any tightening pressure applied to them is translated into outward pressure on the material, almost guaranteeing some eventual cracking.

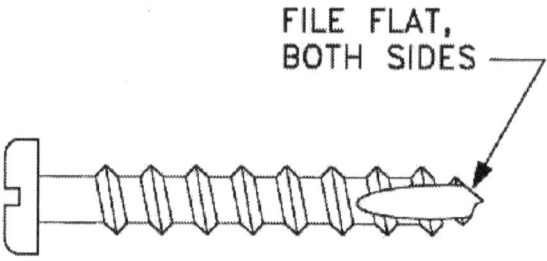

Figure 20-4
A sheet-metal screw modified to act as a tapping die.

A few mores notes about self-tapping screws: If you're threading a long screw into a thick panel or have chosen to reduce the size of the pilot hole to provide additional grip, you can easily modify the screw to provide some thread-forming capability and make its installation easier and safer. Clamp the screw in a vise or hold it with a pair of pliers and file away some of the threads to form a flat area near the tip as shown in Figure 4. This creates cutting edges which will remove material and form crude threads as you insert the screw. Turn the screw over and file a matching flat on the opposite side to double the number of cutting edges and insure that the screw will remain on center in the pilot hole.

When installing any screw, always squirt some silicone caulking into the pilot hole and apply a bit to the screw before installing it. In addition to sealing the fiberglass and helping to lock the screw in place, the silicone lubricates the screw as it's threaded in.

Finally, do your fingers and your boat's finish a favor -- refuse to use anything but Phillips-head screws. Slotted-head screws encourage the screwdriver to slip sideways at the most inopportune times. Phillips-head screws retain the screwdriver's business end and, if you use the correct size for the screw head, will help you drive the screw in straighter.

Large Clearance Holes

Most of the caveats and precautions discussed above hold true for large clearance holes. The exception is the absence of any threads in the hole because they'll be sized to allow free passage of their respective fastener or accessory. There are added considerations, however. The use of large-diameter twist drills (1/4" and up) in fiberglass becomes more of a problem as the size increases. They tend to chatter during the cutting process, greatly increasing the chance of chipping or cracking the fiberglass. Also, because the FRP is so much softer than the metals they were designed to cut, they tend to dig in or self-engage to the point where the drill actually gets drawn in so quickly that it will either stall or plunge through the panel. Either case will almost certainly result in damage to the surrounding area.

The tool of choice then is a rotary hole saw. The smaller ones will operate quite nicely in the average hand drill as long as it's equipped with a 3/8" or 1/2" chuck. Most are equipped with a pilot drill to help in locating them as they bore. Used carefully, they do a great job.

To protect against scratches and digs, generously cover the area to be modified with a layer or two of masking tape. Mark the center of the intended hole and then drill a pilot hole slightly smaller than the pilot drill of the hole saw. Then cut the main hole. When it's complete, gently peel off the masking tape by pulling it towards the center of the hole.

Chances are that the hole you've cut will be too large to be chamfered with a countersink, but the edge still must be beveled to protect the gel-coat. This can be done with a fine half-round file or medium-grit sandpaper, but it must be done with downward strokes only, pushing down against the gel-coat, not drawing up against its edge. Seal the edge of the FRP by wiping some silicone around it with your finger and you're done.

Large Gaping Holes

Most of us won't have occasion to put a really large hole in our boat, and that's fortunate because it presents the greatest opportunity to do something you'll regret later. But since the First Mate expects an opening hatch over the V-berth, let's get to it.

In most cases, large holes will not be round but rather square or rectangular in shape. This presents a problem right away because an opening of this size has the potential of creating structural weaknesses, and if it has square corners, the results will show up there. As a structural entity, a boat is subjected to enormous stress. Think about the teeth-loosening landing you survived after launching *Superscow* off the crest of a six-foot wave last week. When those stresses are transmitted to the panel with the hole in it, they will be concentrated at the corners, and you'll find cracks propagating from those corners in no time at all. The same holds true for any sharp irregularities in the edge of the opening.

The good news is that the potential for these problems is easily avoided. The secret is an oxymoron: round corners. Corners of the opening should have the maximum radius that the installation will allow, and the entire edge of the opening should be as smooth and regular as you can make it. The radii (radiuses, if you insist) will evenly distribute the stresses to adjacent areas rather than allow them to concentrate dangerously at the corners. The potential for cracking will be greatly reduced.

The weapon of choice for this operation is the humble sabre-saw equipped with a fine-tooth metal-cutting blade. If a tight corner radius is required, it may be tighter than the saw's turning radius. (The narrower the blade, front-to-back, the tighter the radius you can cut.) If so, consider using a rotary hole saw to form the corner contours, then cut out the remainder of the plug with the saw. Either way, begin by applying a generous swath of masking tape along the cutting path. This will protect the boat's finish from the saw's shoe and reduce the gel-coat's natural tendency to chip during the cutting operation. You can mark the outline of the hole right on the tape. If you're not using a hole saw for the corners, drill a starter hole for the sabre-saw just inside the cut line. Once the cutting is complete, remove the tape by pulling it toward the center of the hole and then chamfer the hole edge as discussed above.

Keep in mind that the First Mate's happiness with the new hatch may be somewhat diminished if you fill the V-berth with fiberglass dust and chips during the installation. You can avoid this unpleasantness by attaching a plastic sheet or trash bag to the backside of the work area with duct tape. (Let it drape loosely so you won't cut it with the saw.) It will collect the offending debris and allow you to dispose of it neatly when you're through.

Having raised the dust issue, here are two important notes about working with fiberglass. Its residue is particularly nasty stuff consisting of resin dust and microscopic rods of glass fiber. Go to great lengths to keep it out of your eyes and lungs because your body is ill-equipped to get rid of it. Keep handy a portable vacuum and a damp rag to collect or wipe up debris as you create it. And then there's the itch part. A dusting of those microscopic glass rods on the skin makes most of us long to lather up in a nice hot shower. Don't do it. Old-timers will tell you that the heat will cause your pores to open up, which only allows the irritant to penetrate deeper and stay longer. Rinse first in the coldest water you can stand, then satisfy your longing to lather.

Backing Plate Tricks

Mounting heavy equipment or accessories such as cleats that will be exposed to high loads requires extra attention to ensure that the loads are well distributed. When the host material is fiberglass, the best way of doing the job is to use a backing plate to prevent the hardware from pulling through the fiberglass and spread the load out over a larger area. Sometimes that's easier said than done.

I ran into such a problem when I needed to install midships cleats on my boat. Because they'd be used for spring lines as well as fenders, I wanted to make sure they were supported by backing plates for strength. The problem was that, although I had access to where the backing plates had to go, I couldn't reach that spot.

After a bit of head-scratching, I solved the problem. I started by using a hacksaw to cut the backing plates out of some scrap steel. Then I used the cleat as a template to mark the position of mounting holes in the gunwale and the backing plate. I drilled and tapped threaded holes into the backing plate to match the mounting screws. (If you don't have access to taps or have to use an aluminum backing plate, you can epoxy four nuts to the underside of backing plate instead. Be sure to follow the epoxy manufacturer's instructions and allow sufficient curing time before use.)

I took a length of sturdy twine and fished its ends down through diagonally opposite gunwale holes, out through the access port and down through corresponding holes in the backing plate, tying the ends together securely under the plate. (See Figure 5.) After thoroughly coating the top of the plate with marine adhesive, I used the twine to draw the plate up into position under the gunwale holes, then pulled it aside and out of the way. Keeping tension on the twine to keep the plate in place, I attached the cleat by installing two of its screws into the open holes. (Don't skimp on the length of the screws. Long ones will make the job easier.) When I was sure they were threaded in properly, but without tightening them up, I cut the cord and withdrew it from below. Then I installed the other two screws, leaving all of them loose enough so I could raise up the cleat to squirt marine sealant under it to seal the drilled holes. Then I fully tightened the screws and cleaned up the excess sealant that had oozed out.

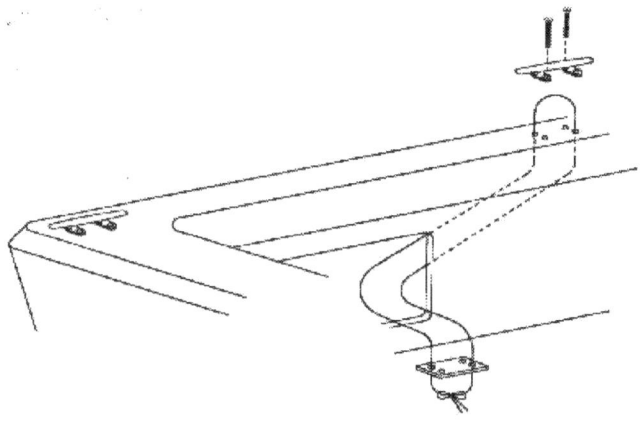

Figure 20-5
Snaking a backing plate into a remote position.

Modern Boatworks -- By David S. Yetman

Chapter Twenty-One
Freshwater Systems

It's a beautiful day on a calm sea and the fish are biting like crazy. You've just reeled in a 12-pounder and sent him flopping into the fishwell. You replace the bait with a smelly, half-rotted chunk of mackerel that's sure to keep your hookup string alive. With hands that look like you've just finished a double shift at a slaughterhouse, you get your gear back into the water just in time for the First Mate to announce that lunch is ready.

It sure would be nice to have a place to wash up.

Even if you prefer to cruise in relative cleanliness instead of messing up your boat with fish offal, a freshwater system is one of the most convenient amenities you can have aboard. Washing sticky hands, showering off saltwater or sand, rinsing out a cup or just cleaning tools in fresh water are simple conveniences that we take for granted ashore but are unavailable to many boaters. But just because many small boats aren't available with pressurized fresh-water systems doesn't mean you can't have and enjoy one on yours, regardless of its size.

My first boat, a 22-foot walkaround, came with a mini-galley equipped with a sink the size of a paperback book and a pump-it-yourself faucet that drew from a two-gallon collapsible container in the compartment below. The container not only collapsed during its first rough outing but broke its plastic connector and emptied itself on the cuddy cabin floor as well. Then the faucet broke in half when I tried to remove it. I wanted to send the whole rig back to the boat's manufacturer, but they had shown great anticipation by going out of business right after they sold me the boat. I was on my own but determined to have water, even if it ended up being just a single outlet and a tiny tank.

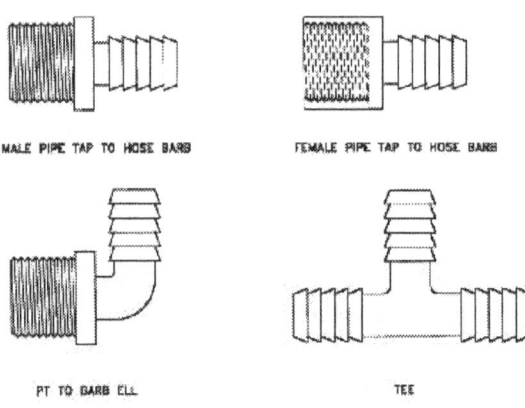

Figure 21-1
Typical hose fittings.

The boat was basically a day-tripper (even though we slept on it occasionally), so I didn't need to carry more than five or six gallons, and I was willing to do without hot water to keep it simple. This meant I only had to find room for a small tank, an electric pump, a filler inlet and passages to run flexible water lines to their destinations (a piece of cake except for the tank). Most of the commercially available tanks are rectangular, while most nooks and crannies on a boat are not. I was fortunate to find enough room under the cockpit sole for two off-the-shelf six-gallon tanks (the next size up, a single 10, was the wrong shape). I mounted the pump in the now-empty compartment under the sink, put a filler inlet in the gunwale just aft of the helm and a tank vent just below it in the topsides. While I was at it, I also converted one of the baitwells in the transom to a sink with a faucet and a retractable spray head on a six-foot hose. The result was a boat that was so much more enjoyable that we soon got tired of hearing each other remark what a good idea the freshwater system was.

While such an installation may sound like a major undertaking, it really wasn't. Most of the work was straightforward for a boater with a fair knowledge of tools and hardware.

Preparation

Plan, plan, plan. Make a sketch, no matter how crude, of your proposed system. Browse through the plumbing sections of your local marine/hardware store to see what bits and pieces are available. Identify the main parts you intend to use, note what each one will require in order to be connected into the system, and write that information on your sketch. Unless you're very ambitious and have lots of time, you'll probably want to use flexible plastic tubing to get the water where you want it. After you've identified all such hardware requirements (and have decided to proceed), the last thing you should do before making any holes in your boat is to assemble the entire system at home to ensure you haven't missed something. Then disassemble it and head for the boat.

Modern Boatworks -- By David S. Yetman

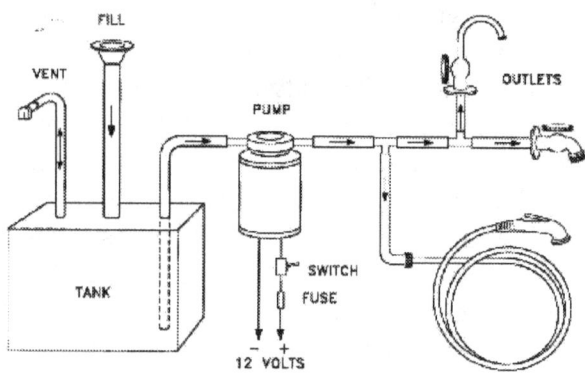

Figure 21-2

Layout for a pressurized fresh water system.

The Tank

The tank should have a fairly large diameter inlet (1" is common) and provisions for attaching smaller vent and outlet hoses. The installation will be much simpler if you can find space for a ready-made tank. Marine stores carry or can get many shapes and sizes with pre-threaded provisions for all the connections. They also have flexible bladder-type tanks that are easier to stuff into odd spaces, but they're quite expensive and are subject to puncture by sharp objects. Be creative when looking for a space to put a tank; it doesn't have to go in the bilge or below the sole. Many small boats have lots of unused space up in the bow or under rod racks in the gunwales. Boats with an I/O drive often have cavernous spaces just forward of the transom. Front-to-back folding seats may have a storage area underneath that will serve the purpose. A small tank will even fit under the athwartship seat of an open boat. You probably won't want to use the water from this system for drinking, so you don't have to be too fussy about using a nontraditional container as a tank if that makes your job easier. If you're familiar with the "stitch and glue" method of boatbuilding, you can even make your own fiberglass tank. Once you've found a spot, mount the tank or wedge it into place very securely. With water weighing more than eight pounds per gallon, it will be heavy when filled.

The Pump

Most marine freshwater pumps have an on-demand feature. They can be left on full-time and will only begin pumping when they detect the drop in system pressure that occurs when a faucet is opened. Many come with quick-disconnect inlet and outlet hose barbs that make them a snap to install. They'll work in almost any position, although their job will be easier if they're not too far above tank level. They should be connected to the boat's 12-volt electrical system through a fuse and a switch so they can be shut off during periods of inactivity or in case of a leak.

Inlet and Vent

If the tank is placed in an inaccessible location, a remote filler is necessary. Filler inlet fixtures are available in several types and sizes. I would not recommend the type to which a garden hose attaches; the high waterline pressure can damage your system. The most convenient placement is in the gunwale surface if you have room, easy to install and convenient to use. They will require that you drill a fairly large hole, which can be made using a rotary hole saw in an electric drill. Ensure that there is adequate access behind the area you choose and that no wiring or cables will be damaged during the process. The large-diameter filler tubing should be run so that it's as free as possible of kinks or sharp bends.

A tank vent line is required to allow air to pass in and out of the tank while filling or draining. Through-hull vent fittings are inexpensive and require only a single hole for installation. Remember that the tank vents at the top and feeds from the bottom. If it's properly vented, its fill inlet can be anywhere, but at the top is best.

Outlets

Water outlets come in as many shapes and sizes as there are uses for them, but the basic ones are bulkhead-mounted, counter-mounted for galley use, and spray-head types for rinsing and showers. If you can justify or find room for only one, make it a spray head on a flexible hose, the most useful of the bunch. Any of them will require a fairly large mounting hole and, again, the rotary hole saw is the right tool for sizes from one inch and up. Smaller sizes between 3/8" and 1" can be drilled in wood or fiberglass using a flat-bladed wood bore in an electric drill. Location of the outlets will depend on how you're going to use them and where you can find room, but using a baitwell as a sink is like having your cake and eating it too; it can still be used as a baitwell when you're not using it as a sink.

Installing even a simple water system on a small boat takes some forethought and resourcefulness, but it isn't an insurmountable task. Once you've done your homework, drilled a few oversize holes in the boat and mounted a few components, the whole system is held together with simple hose clamps. The bottom line is that it pays off handsomely in convenience every time you use the boat, and again in resale value when it's time to move up.

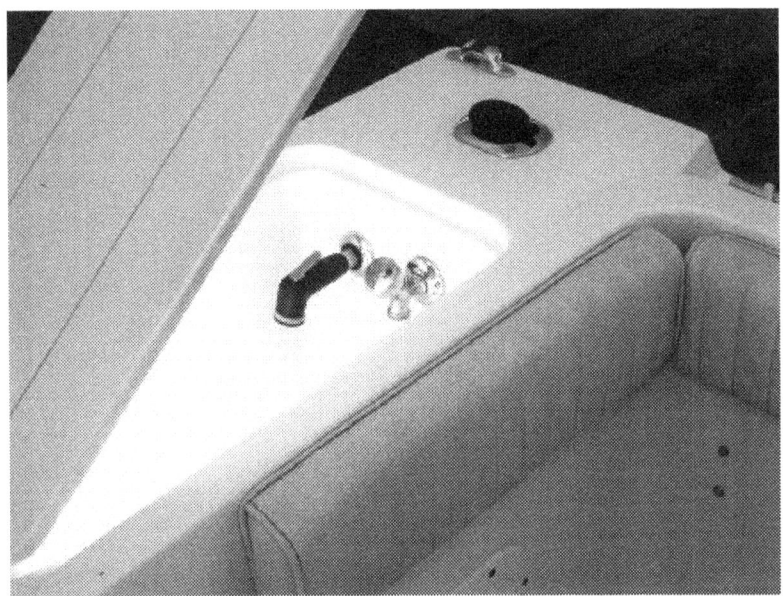

Figure 21-3

This bait well has been converted to a handy sink complete with shower hose.

Modern Boatworks -- *By David S. Yetman*

Chapter Twenty-Two
Washdown Systems

The good news is that the big ones have been biting like crazy and your fishwells are full. The bad news is that the cockpit looks like the back room of a fish market: fish scales everywhere, mud on the coaming pads, chum clogging the scuppers, and the place smells like a landfill. Since you don't have a raw-water washdown system, you have a choice of forming a bucket brigade or waiting until you get back to the marina to clean up. Some choice.

Many manufacturers of small boats (and some larger ones) don't bother to install raw-water washdown systems on their products. It's a way to hold down costs, and not everyone needs one anyway, but that's no reason to do without. You can install a washdown system quickly and inexpensively on almost any boat, and in some cases, you can have one without even bothering to install it. The only caveat is that your boat should be large enough to be self-bailing.

Washdown systems are relatively simple, consisting of an electrically operated pump, an inlet for raw water, and an outlet connection for a hose. The pumps are usually positive-displacement diaphragm types which have a built-in pressure sensor to switch themselves off when the outlet line pressure exceeds a pre-set point so they only run when needed. The inlet is usually a through-hull fitting below the water line with a shut-off valve called a seacock, which allows the inlet be closed when it's not in use. The outlet side of the pump is connected to a faucet threaded to accept a garden hose and mounted in the cockpit wall. Flexible plastic hoses are used to connect the washdown system components to each other.

One of the perceived drawbacks of installing a washdown system is the need to drill a hole in the hull below the water line for the water inlet, because a leaking or broken through-hull fitting has the potential for sinking the boat. That's a valid concern, so installation should be done carefully, but with a bit of clever plumbing, an inlet below the waterline is unnecessary on many boats.

The first step is to plan the location of the components. Location of the pump is important because most of the work is centered around it. It should be in a relatively accessible, dry, out-of-the-way place. Behind a cockpit wall under the gunwale is common, since many boats have easily removable rod-holder inserts in the cockpit sides to provide easy access. It also allows a very short run for the outlet plumbing because the faucet can be mounted on the same wall. Most pumps are supplied with inlet and outlet barbs, which will determine the hose size. All hose connections to the pump and in the outlet plumbing should be made with hose clamps.

The best position for the water inlet, in spite of the potential problems and expense, is in the hull below the water line. If you decide to go this route, don't scrimp on the quality of the hardware because safety is involved. Use a bronze through-hull fitting that incorporates a built-in shut-off. Opt for reinforced rubber inlet hose instead of plastic, and double-clamp it to the seacock. The inlet's location should be placed to ensure that the turbulence it creates won't affect depth sounder or speedometer sensors that may be mounted aft of it.

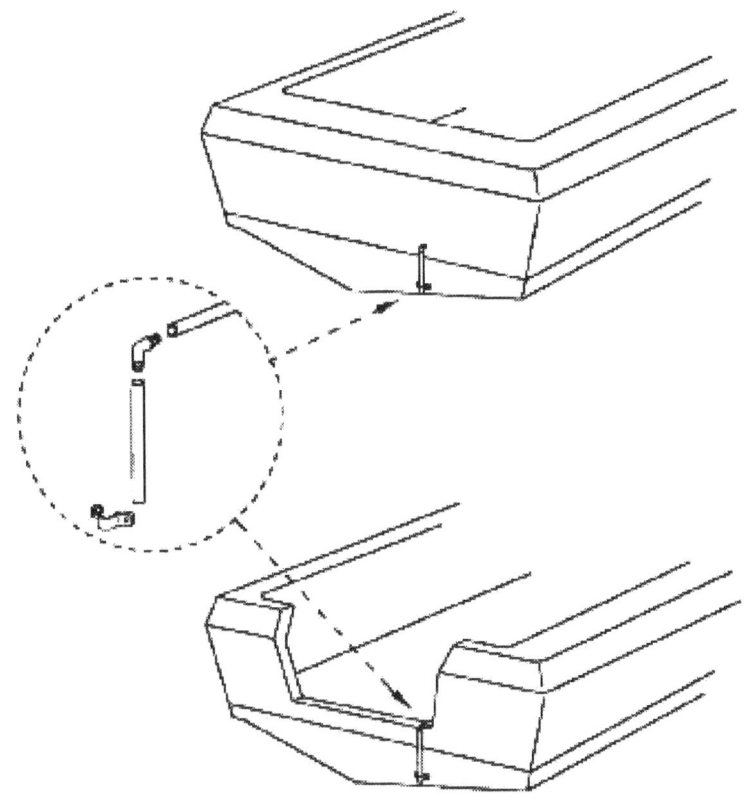

Figure 22-1
Alternate locations for raw water inlets.

An alternate arrangement, although it still requires a hole in the boat, is to drill through the transom above the water line, and install the inlet hose as shown at the top of Figure 1. While this doesn't eliminate the trauma of drilling a large hole in your boat, it can reduce the possibility of sinking if a leak develops. In many cases you'll be able to position the hose under the swim platform or next to other hardware so it won't be obvious. On fiberglass or wooden boats, the hole can be made using a paddle-shaped wood-boring bit in an electric drill and should be just large enough to accommodate the hose. Drill a small pilot hole all the way through, then drill the full-size hole half way from each side to avoid damaging the gel coat. Install the hose using a right-angle barb to turn the corner and direct the hose downward. Use a plastic "U" clamp (available in most hardware stores) to keep the hose in place. Make sure the hose doesn't extend below the lower edge of the hull. The hose-to-barb connections on the un-pressurized intake line shouldn't need clamps if you've used a barb that matches the hose size. The hole through the transom should be very well sealed on both sides with a liberal application of marine sealant designed to be used below the waterline to prevent moisture from causing internal damage to the transom core.

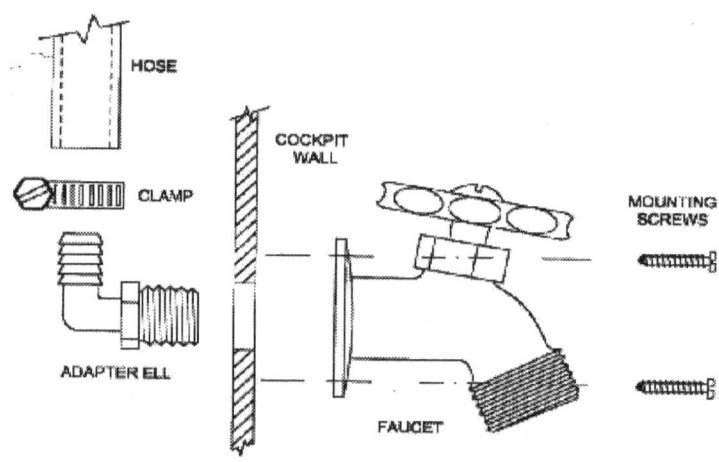

Figure 22-2
Mounting a washdown outlet.

Installation is even easier on outboard boats because the need to drill a hole is eliminated; you can just run the hose over the top of the transom cut-out as shown in the lower half of Figure 1. The only drawback is that the system may not work well while you're under way due to air being sucked into the inlet, so you'll have to clean up before you get under way.

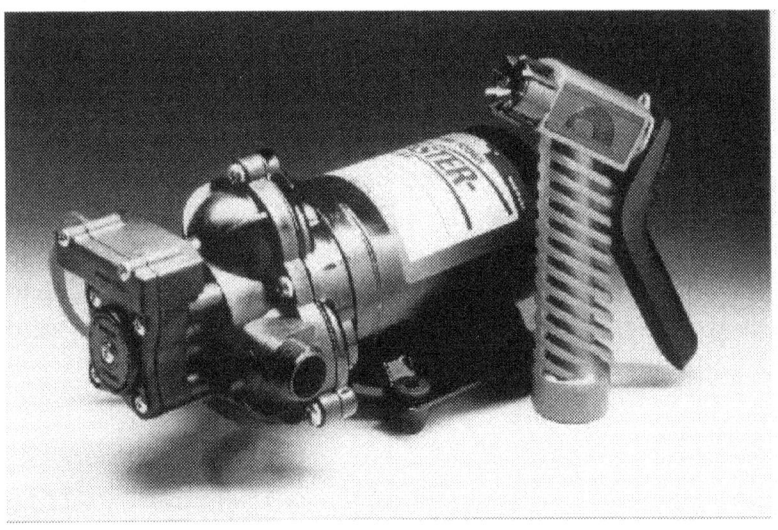

Figure 22-3
Courtesy of ShurFlo Pump Mfg Co.
The pump and nozzle supplied as a washdown kit.

The outlet is largely a matter of taste and budget. Several pump manufacturers such as the Shurflo offer washdown kits that eliminate some of the fuss of installation because the outlet hose can be attached directly to the pump. The other approach is to use an outlet mounted in the cockpit wall as shown in Figure 2. Home-improvement stores (where they're called sillcocks) sell a plastic one for under $3 or a bronze one for under $7. Either will be available with a female-thread inlet and prove to be virtually maintenance- and corrosion-free. If stainless steel or chrome plating is more attractive to you, a marine store will fill your need for up to $50. Connect the pump's outlet hose to the faucet using an adapter that has a hose barb on one end and a male thread to match the faucet on the other. Remember that the mounting hole for the outlet will have to be large enough to clear the hose adapter. All connections in the pressurized side of the system should be made using rugged, stainless steel hose clamps. Figure 4 is a simplified system diagram.

The electrical connection should be made using the wire size suggested by the pump manufacturer, or in the absence of a recommendation, with at least #14 wire. The hot (red) line should go to a switch and then to a fuse. The black wire goes to ground. Although the pump will shut itself off when not used, it's still a good idea to be able to switch it off when unattended or the system springs a leak.

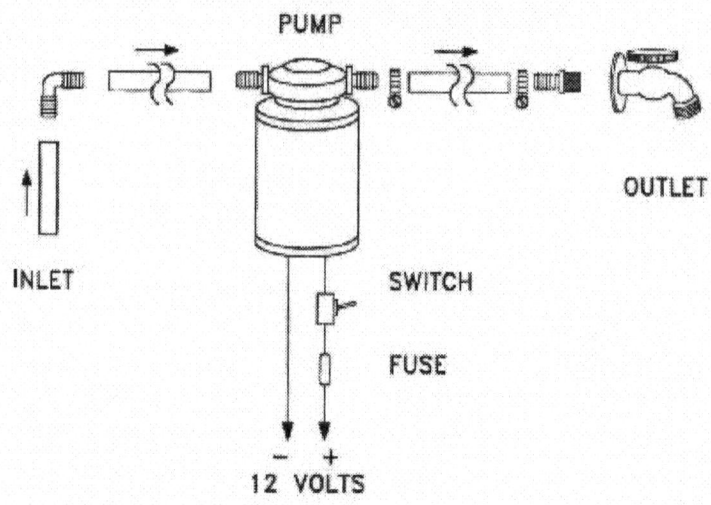

Figure 22-4
Diagram of a raw-water washdown system.

A washdown system that needs no installation is the $30 brainchild of one of my marina neighbors. He bought a submersible bilge pump, attached 20 feet of hose to its outlet and added a long cord with a cigarette lighter plug to its electrical wiring. Using small-diameter line, he tied the hose and the wire together about three feet above the pump and left a loop in the line. At washdown time, he lowers the pump into the water, hooks the loop over a cleat and plugs the rig into his lighter adapter. He doesn't get blasting pressure but has more than enough flow to wash down smartly.

A Handy Scrubbing Tool

One of the conveniences of a raw-water washdown system is the ability to hose down the topsides and waterline. The clean-up of the river where I dock is still a work in progress, so I need to scrub the waterline more often than I'd like. After a bit of experimenting, I came up with a simple yet effective tool that allows me to do the scrubbing from the deck.

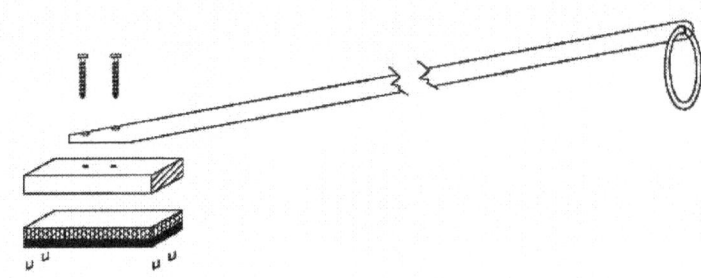

Figure 22-5

A handy scrubbing tool.

I cut a block of wood to match the size of a 3"x5" scouring sponge, the type meant for scrubbing nonstick cookware. Then I cut the end of a broomstick at a very shallow angle, drilled two holes in it and attached it to the wood block with stainless-steel screws. (See Figure 5.) After wetting the sponge to make it pliable, I attached it to the block with builder's staples at each corner (carpet tacks will do as well). The staples or tacks remain well below the surface and are not a danger to the finish. Finally, I drilled a hole in the other end of the broomstick for a loop of shock cord as a strap to go around my wrist so I won't lose it overboard.

    The scouring sponge is easy to replace as it wears out. Just pry the staples out and attach the replacement, but be sure to use one that's intended for plastic or nonstick cookware. Anything else will severely damage the paint or gel-coat.

Modern Boatworks -- By David S. Yetman

Chapter Twenty-Three
Build a Folding Foot Rest

It would be a rare boat that came with all the conveniences you want and had them placed exactly where you need them. But even if you reached that happy state, you'd run into another problem: tripping all over them because of the lack of space. Many builders get around such limitations by designing ingenious, self-stowing accessories like tables, bunks and seats into their boats. Dinette tables that lower to become part of the V-berth and fold-down jump seats are good examples.

Another area that can benefit from this type of thinking is the helm, where foot rests are often absent, misplaced or in the way. Most skippers alternate between standing and sitting, depending on conditions, so a sturdy foot rest that folds out of the way when not needed can add to convenience, comfort and safety.

The foot rest platform and its support legs can be simple shapes cut from marine plywood or constructed more elegantly from teak or oak like the example shown in Figure 1. The hardware on the example consists of a small cabinet latch, two pairs of stainless-steel hinges, a tie bar and a pivot that can be made from do-it-yourself material available at hardware stores. The tie bar shown was made from 1/8" aluminum, which is easy to drill and can be cut and shaped quite easily using a sabre saw equipped with a metal-cutting blade. The resulting rough edges can be smoothed with a file and coarse sandpaper.

The tie bar pivot was made from a short piece of aluminum angle. Both the tie bar and its pivot can also be made from oak or teak, but they may not be as durable or compact as their metal counterparts.

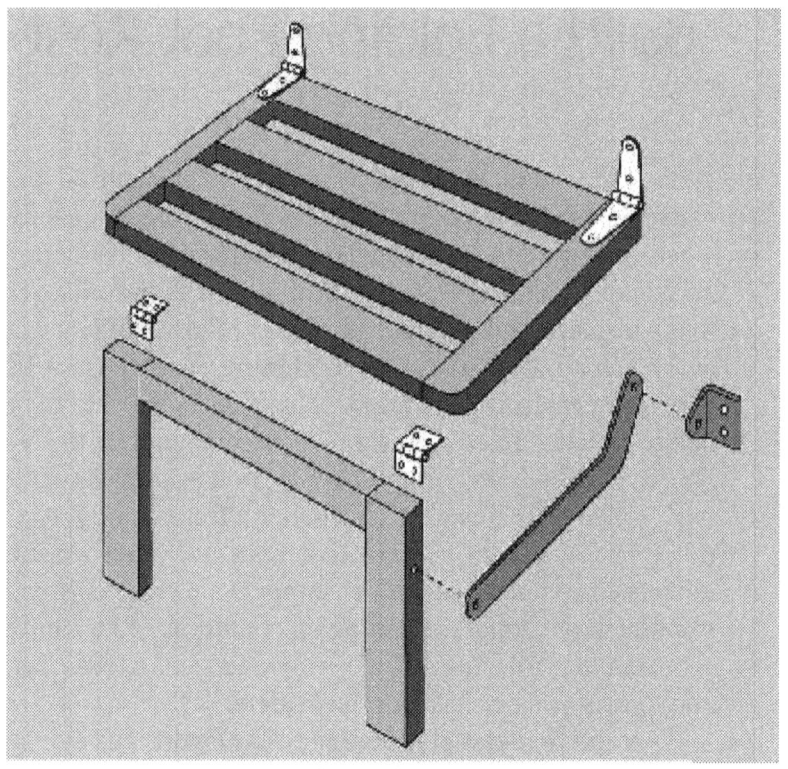

Figure 23-1
The parts of a folding footrest.

The tie bar is an integral part of the folding mechanism. Its purpose is to ensure that the legs are extended and held in the proper support position when the foot rest is in use and to retract the legs when the unit is folded up. The spring-loaded cabinet latch is used to keep the footrest securely in its upright position. While the folding mechanism may look complex at first, it's easy to plan and will work flawlessly if one simple two-part rule is followed. As shown in Figure 2, dimension A1 must be the same as A2. And dimension B1 must be the same as B2 so that the four pivot points become the corners of a parallelogram. Other than retaining its dog-leg shape (to clear the platform when it's folded), the shape of the tiebar is not important to the mechanism's geometry as long as its pivot points are the correct distance apart.

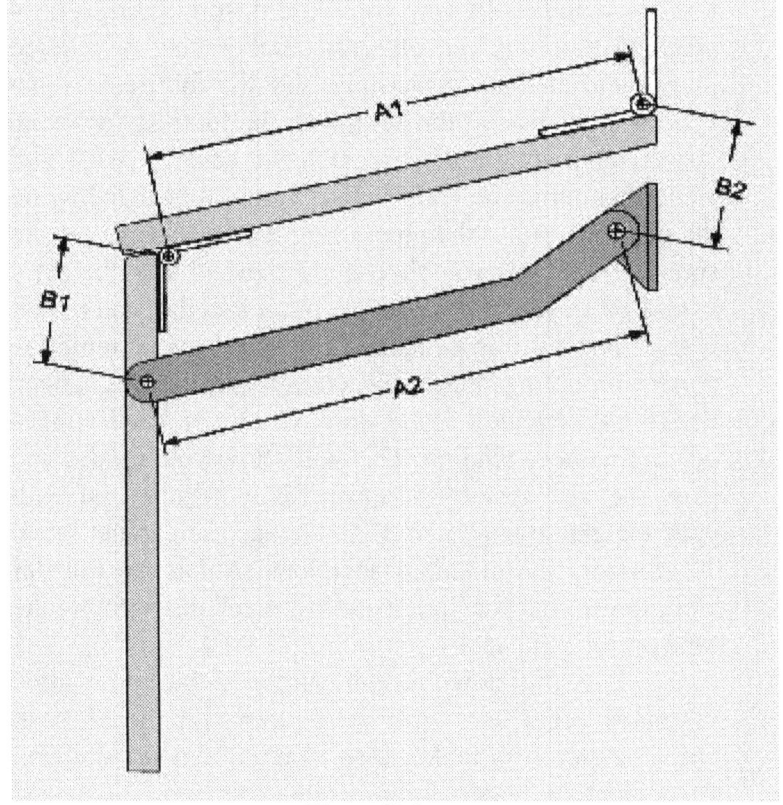

Figure 23-2

The geometry of the mechanism of a folding footrest.

The tie bar pivot and the cabinet latch can be mounted to the bulkhead with #6 self-tapping screws. The hinges should be attached to the foot rest and to the bulkhead with the largest screw size possible (#10 at a minimum). Keep in mind that self-tapping screws require a properly sized pilot hole when used in fiberglass. It's also prudent to bevel the edge of the hole to prevent gelcoat chipping and to ease the entry of the screw with a dab of silicone as a lubricant and sealer.

It's important that the size and position of the foot rest are suited to the way you'll use it, so building a free-standing mock-up out of scrap lumber may be a good investment of time. If possible, size the foot rest so that you can still stand at the helm with the footrest deployed. Use it for a couple of days to make sure it's what you want, then build the real thing. If you will be standing on the platform rather than just using it as a foot rest, make sure the materials you choose are sized to take the extra load. Before you apply a finish, put it together and mount it to a shop wall or a piece of plywood to determine the correct mounting points and ensure that the mechanism works as planned. Make sure the pivots and hinges operate without binding. This will allow you to raise and stow the foot rest by simply lifting the platform with your toe and swinging it up to engage the cabinet latch. Then record the mounting locations so you can transfer them to the boat for final installation and disassemble the footrest for finishing.

This fold-down design can be scaled up or down for many other uses such as a jump seat, bench seat, boarding step or a table. Keep in mind that the size and strength of the material and hardware should be adjusted to match the intended use, especially where personal safety is involved.

Figure 23-3
The footrest in position for use.

Figure 23-4
The footrest can be folded up out of the way.

Figure 23-5

A simple cabinet latch holds the folded footrest in place.

Chapter Twenty-Four
Customizing Your Instrument Panel

Outfitting a new boat with electronics or installing new instruments in your present one can be a frustrating experience. There's rarely enough room to do exactly what you want, so the outcome usually involves a compromise unless you are willing to start from scratch. In many cases, it's the right way to go. Making a decision to tear out the control center of your boat may be a frightening thought, but having survived that, the real challenge is to come up with a workable plan. The old carpenter's advice to measure twice and cut once was never more meaningful. The basic plan should have three parts: make sure the devices you want to install will physically fit; identify and check the availability of the tools and materials required; study the surroundings of the area you intend to use for the new layout (and the space behind it) so there'll be no surprises later.

The simplest thing to do is to cut out an exact-size cardboard replica of the panel area, make full-size, two-dimensional replicas of the accessories you want to install and shuffle them around until you find an arrangement that will work. Another way is to use drawing or drafting software on a computer to come up with a dimensioned drawing of the new layout as shown in Figure 1. If you're patient, you can also accomplish the same thing with a full-size manual drawing. However you choose, make sure your models represent the true area in front of and behind the panel, that the real part will fit the finished product.

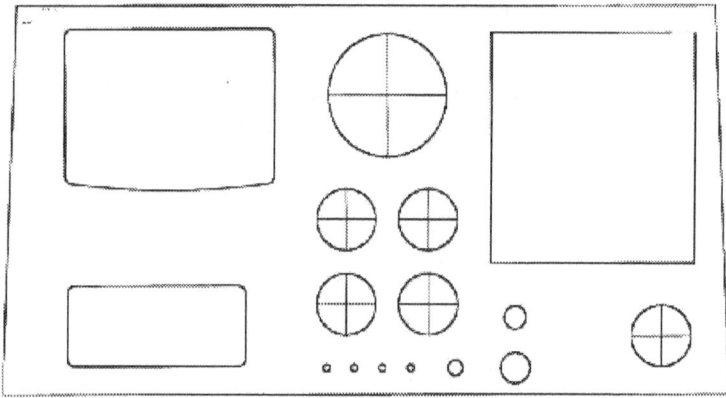

Figure 24-1
The plan for making an instrument panel.

Tools and material choices are less straightforward because they will depend on the individual situation. Whether the present setup has a removable panel or not, a new one will be required to accommodate the revised arrangement. Unless you're fortunate enough to have access to a metal-working shop, plastic is the material of choice for the panel. A 1/4" thick laminate such as Garolite XX is strong and moisture-resistant, but any workable plastic sheet except acrylic (which is very brittle) can be used. Sheet plastic should be available in most areas; many will even cut the piece exactly to size for you. Plastic can be worked with ordinary tools in most cases. Holes for things like meters can be formed with a rotary hole saw or, if you have access to a drill press, more easily with an inexpensive, adjustable fly-cutter. Large, square or odd-shaped cutouts for other instruments can be made with a saber saw.

When you've determined that the job is feasible, begin by drawing a rough sketch of the existing layout that identifies the present accessories and their position. Then label every single wire connection before beginning the disassembly. Self-adhesive labels which have been cut into small strips make good markers. Once the existing instruments have been removed, you'll have better visual access for double-checking that there will be room enough behind the panel for the instruments in their new positions.

Figure 24-2
The instrument panel "before" modification.

If the job still looks do-able, the next step is to put the necessary holes in the new panel. To protect its surface and make marking it easier, cover its face with masking tape. Draw the exact locations and outlines of the holes on the tape, and use them to guide you as you drill and cut out the holes. After removing the tape and sanding the resulting edges, apply a couple of coats of spray paint to the finished panel, then let it bake in the sun for a day or so. The baking isn't a necessity, but it makes the finish much more durable.

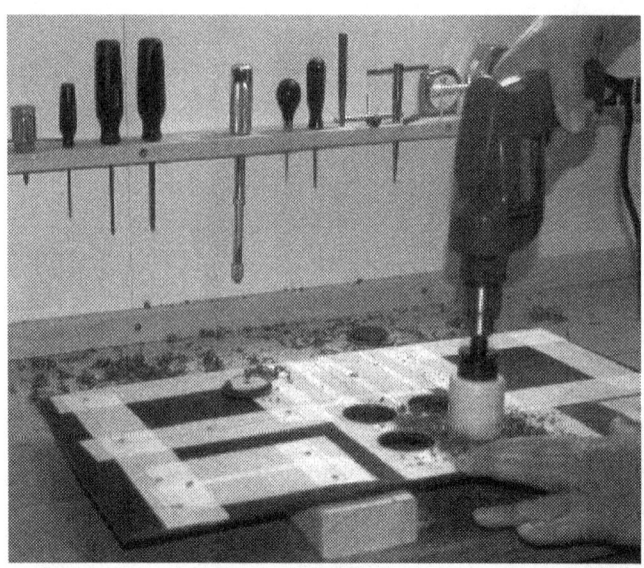

Figure 24-3
Using a hole saw to ct round holes in the new panel.

    By temporarily mounting the new panel in position you'll be able to mark any areas of the boat's structure that interfere with the new arrangement and then remove them with the saber saw. The instruments can then be mounted.

You'll be surprised at how much of the existing wiring you'll be able to re-route to the new layout, although you may have to un-bundle the cable harnesses to do so. For instances where there isn't enough length, you can make longer wires from wire and crimp-on terminals available at the local marine store. Be sure to use wire specifically manufactured for marine use.

Figure 24-4

Using a saber saw to create large openings in the panel.

Anything less will corrode and cause trouble when you need it least. Where it isn't possible to replace a wire, lengthen the old one by cutting and splicing a new center section of equal or larger size. Solder the joints and wrap them securely with electrician's tape. The final step is to connect up the new instruments, then re-bundle the wires into a harness using nylon cable ties. Tying the wires together allows them to support each other, greatly reducing flexing and chafe.

Careful planning and marking of connections will be rewarded when you turn on the power and discover that everything works. No smoke, no fire, no loud noises. The best insurance against problems is to spend as much or more time planning the job as you spend in actually doing it. Measure twice; cut once.

Figure 24-5

The finished custom panel.

This quick description of a fairly complex task glosses over the skinned knuckles, the occasional frustration and the sore muscles from working in contorted positions. (Boat designers and manufacturers don't always provide reasonable access to things like panel wiring.) If you approach the task logically and carefully, you don't need to be an electrician or an accomplished mechanic to do the job, but the rewards are worth the effort. Having a helm set up to suit your needs is something you'll enjoy for as long as you own the boat.

Chapter Twenty-Five
Non-Skid Pads

Those of us who trailer our boats often find ourselves walking or standing on the tongue or rails of the trailer during launching or retrieval operations to hook onto the bow-eye or to winch the boat up into place. It's a potentially dangerous situation. The footing can be slippery and the position precarious, but there aren't too many ways to avoid it.

I had a couple of close calls in my early days of trailering. I skinned my shin once on the winch stand, got thoroughly wet on another occasion but was fortunate to avoid serious injury to anything but my pride. (These things always happen in front of a crowd.) In the back of my mind I kept thinking about ways to improve my odds, but I never got around to doing anything about it.

Then one day I found myself watching another guy retrieve his boat. He was very careful, stepping from one side of the trailer to the other to make sure the hull was correctly positioned on the rollers. H was headed back to the winch when he lost his footing and fell awkwardly between the rails of the trailer. His injuries were painful, though luckily not serious, but the episode stuck in my mind and made me determined not to repeat his experience.

At first I thought it might be possible to launch and retrieve without actually standing on the trailer, but I still had to get from one side to the other, which required me to at least climb over the tongue. Trying to operate the winch at chest level is an exercise in futility, and there was no way to avoid getting on the trailer.

My first idea was to apply non-skid paint to the tops of the rails, but many paints don't adhere very well to galvanized surfaces without interim coats of a special primer. Then I thought about using rubber step pads, the kind you see on gunwales, but I would need a number of them to do the job, so it was going to be expensive.

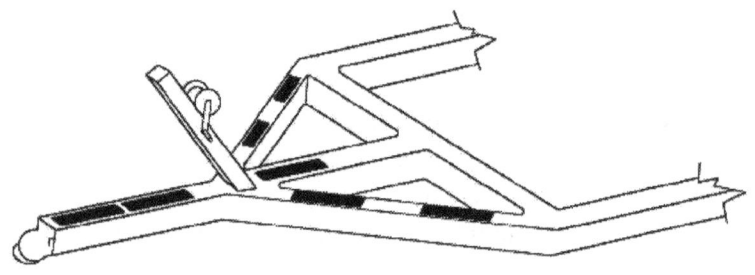

Figure 25-1
Non-skid pads on the trailer rails.

I didn't like the idea of drilling all those holes in the trailer. They were also quite bulky, making them potentially easy to trip on. I finally discovered a quick and easy solution while wandering the aisles of the local home-improvement center. People who climb ladders need the same safe, secure footing as boaters who dance around on trailers. The ingenious 3M Corp. offers self-adhesive step-ladder treads made from a flexible material that has the look and feel of coarse sandpaper and provides very secure footing, even under water. It's available in pre-cut pads that can be used as is or cut and shaped to suit. The pads are about 2"x9".

They turned out to be just the right width for the rails of my trailer. I cleaned the galvanized surface free of dirt and grease before applying the pads to the rails wherever I might need to stand. They worked like a charm. The trailer is on its second owner now, and the pads are still there. They've stood up very well for several years, providing a durable, inexpensive solution to a potentially dangerous situation.

The idea worked so well that I went looking for other uses. One was on the teak swim platform. I used to go to great lengths to keep it looking shipshape, sanding it down and re-oiling it every spring, all of which left it with a nice and smooth finish. Unfortunately, that made it very slippery; swimmers coming aboard had to be very careful to climb over the transom. Strategically placed handgrips made it only slightly less dangerous.

I thought it was perfect place for more of the non-skid pads until I accidentally knelt on one. The material's coarse texture made it very uncomfortable, and it would be even worse for a youngster's tender skin, so it was out of the question.

Luckily, a clerk at the home-improvement store had mentioned another possibility: non-skid strips for bathtubs and showers. They have a much finer texture and very easy to cut into smaller pieces. Their liberal application to the teak slats ahead of the swim ladder makes the platform a much safer place to be.

Modern Boatworks -- By David S. Yetman

Chapter Twenty-Six
Get a Grip

If you watch closely as people boards a boat, you'll see them concentrate on two things: carefully watch their footing, then instinctively look for something to hold on to. It's not just landlubbers who do it; even experienced mariners are often more comfortable with a grab rail in hand.

Boats can be an unstable, unpredictable platform for humans who depend on a keen sense of balance to remain upright and retain their decorum, so we compensate for the instability by holding onto whatever is handy. Most boats offer lots of places to grasp. A well-designed boat will have handles and grab rails placed exactly where they're needed every time. Unfortunately, many don't fall into that category, so owners must figure out where and how to mount handles and grab rails for convenience and safety.

Safety is the primary concern. When you fall on a boat, you have more chances to be injured than if you fell ashore, and that's assuming you stay on the boat. A man-overboard incident is a terrifying situation, but there are plenty of opportunities to prevent them. Just few minutes equipping your boat with a few properly placed hand-holds can make a big difference in safety and everyday convenience. Figure 1 shows common locations for handles and grab rails. Most are so logical that you have

Modern Boatworks -- By David S. Yetman

to wonder why boats don't come with them as standard equipment.

Starting from the stern, you can't have too many hand-holds at or near the swim ladder. A handle on the platform and another on the transom above provide the most functionality as well as a good place to secure floating toys or personal gear. For inboard/outboard boats, a grab handle at the rear of the engine cover has multiple uses. It makes raising the cover much easier and provides purchase for climbing over the transom. In the helm area, hand-holds belong at the point where you'd turn to go forward, at the crew seat (remember that your passenger doesn't have the wheel to hold on to). Speaking of belowdecks, bulkheads and overheads are good places to provide hand-holds as well.

On a walk-around or open boat, almost everyone naturally holds onto the windshield while going forward, but these hand-holds are inaccessible when the enclosure is in place. The need for something to grasp is especially acute on boats with very narrow walkways. The easiest solution is to mount handles to the windshield frame. Even very small ones will offer a steadying point as you go forward. Grab rails mounted to the cabin top can also be helpful, especially on boats with abbreviated or minus bow rails.

I favor large, tubular metal handles whose ends are bent down into an arc that "disappears" into the surface on which they're mounted. These usually have threaded studs welded to them; installing their nuts and washers requires access to the back side of the panel or bulkhead they'll be mounted on. They're available in several lengths, so they can be used as handles or rails. Teak rails generally are attached by external screws threaded into the mounting surface. (Remember that they'll require more maintenance than metal rails.) Most other types will have tabs or flanges that accept flat-head mounting screws to go into or through the panel on which they're mounted.

In choosing a handle or grab rail, opt for the largest you can conveniently use. Large handles are much easier to grasp, are more comfortable to hold and will support a greater load. Consideration of the loads they'll be required to support is also important when deciding how to mount them. A handle above the swim ladder may have to support a large swimmer and should be solidly mounted using through-bolts with backing washers if possible. An alternative would be a handle with four or more mounting screws to spread the load.

In cases where different materials are available, I always go for stainless steel, the longest-lasting, lowest-maintenance choice. Chrome-plated brass or bronze would be next, followed by chrome-plated zinc alloys (the least durable of choices, especially in a salty environment.) Wood and plastic alternatives are acceptable if they're used where their potentially lower strength will not be an issue.

Mounting accessories on your boat should be approached with great care. Fiberglass is easily damaged by improper modification, but the good news is that it's not difficult to do it correctly. Wherever you have access to the reverse side of the panel or bulkhead, use nuts and washers rather than self-tapping screws. Drill the proper size clearance for the screw size you'll use, then bevel its entry with a countersink. The bevel can also be formed with a larger-diameter drill (by hand) if you don't have a countersink, but the bevel is important to keep the gel-coat from cracking.

If you have no rear access and must use self-tapping screws, drilling a correctly sized pilot hole for each screw is essential to avoid damaging the gel-coat and fiberglass.

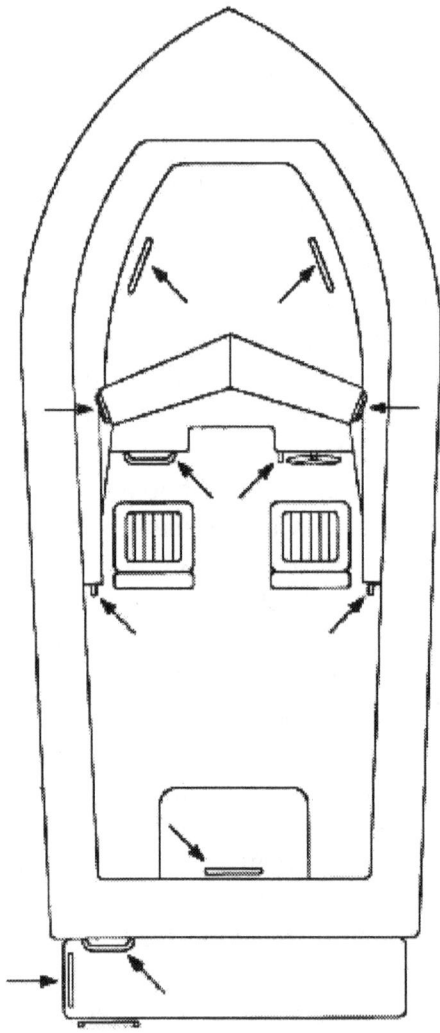

Figure 26-1

Typical locations for handles and grab rails.

Each hole should be beveled as mentioned above to prevent the screw threads from coming in contact with the gel-coat. Squirt a bit of silicone sealer or marine adhesive into each hole before installing. This will lubricate the screw's entry and seal the hole. If you're threading a screw into a panel with a wood or foam core, sealing is particularly important as a moisture barrier. Don't scrimp.

Mounting a handle to a metal windshield frame is a job that should be undertaken with great care. It's imperative to avoid coming into contact with the edge of the windshield glass. It's also important to avoid damaging any wiring that may be embedded in the frame.

Most windshield frames are extrusions. If you were to cut through one, you'd discover a U-shape channel which the glass and its rubber gasket fit into. Adjacent would be a separate channel for wires leading to windshield wipers or running lights. Before drilling into the frame, ensure that you won't come in contact with the glass and that the section of the frame you're drilling into is not being used as a wiring channel.

The location of existing screws provides a good clue. Very often, wiring channels will be covered with a rubber strip or end cap that can be lifted or removed to see what's underneath. Failing that, you can look where the wiring enters the windshield frame to get an idea where it's going. Finally, be very careful about the size of the pilot hole when installing a self-tapping screw in metal. If the hole is too small, it could cause the screw to break off before becoming fully seated.

Adding handles or grab rails is one of the easiest and least expensive ways of upgrading the convenience and safety of your boat. They make the time you and your guests spend afloat more comfortable and add to the value of your boat.

Modern Boatworks -- By David S. Yetman

Chapter Twenty-Seven
The Name Game

Self-adhesive vinyl lettering is one of the best things that modern technology has done for boaters. For those lacking access to capable sign painters, vinyl lettering removes the learning curve and provides the potential for professional-looking results. The cost is affordable, and the application process is easy. But it's not foolproof.

Unless you're an annual boat buyer, applying names isn't something you do very often, so you don't get a lot of practice. Yet, if you charge ahead and do it badly, the result will be prominently displayed for years.

The three most common problems are contamination on the underlying surface that prevents the letters from adhering; improper positioning; and air bubbles remaining under the vinyl.

Removing contamination means getting rid of dirt, scum, oil, polish and wax that have built up on the surface. If the surface is gel-coat, strong solvents such as acetone or paint thinner can be used, but great care should be exercised on painted surfaces where a very strong detergent and hot water may be a better bet. In either case, a soap-and-water wash with a thorough rinse is a good step.

Positioning the lettering correctly requires planning and preparation. Most vinyl products will arrive in the form of a translucent overlay and a protective sheet on the adhesive side, with the vinyl in between. The sheets are not always cut square or even. Making the new cut an inch or so above the lettering will render following steps easier.

Mount the entire "sandwich" in its approximate position on the boat with tabs of masking tape along the top edge to keep it in place. Measure the distance between the top of the letters and some reference point on the boat such as a rub rail, and adjust the position until it's correct. Often it helps to view the results from a distance as well as close-up to ensure that it will look like you'd planned.

Next apply a strip of masking tape along the entire top edge, half on the overlay and half overlapping onto the boat. (Figure 1A) This will create a hinge to allow you to flip the sandwich up without losing its position. The same approach can be used to position free-form graphics, but the positioning will have to be more by eyeball than measurement.

If your lettering is arranged in an arc, and if you were able to order exactly what you wanted, it can be positioned as outlined above. If not, you can easily create your own custom arc from straight lettering. Follow the steps above as if you were going to mount the letters straight, including the tape hinge. Use a pair of scissors to make a cut between each letter as shown in Figure 1B, cutting through both the overlay and the protective sheet, but don't cut all the way up through the tape. Then, leaving the center section taped in place, pull away one side at a time and reposition it in the shape of the desired arc, allowing each letter's sheet to slightly overlap its neighbor. (Figure 1C) If the letters (not the sheets) overlap or are too close because the arc is too tight, put them back to the straight position and turn the process upside down, making a tape hinge at the bottom. The space between the letters will increase when they're fanned out to create the arc. Make sure everything is positioned exactly where you want it before proceeding.

The final step is actually placing the letters in place. Some vinyls can be applied to a surface wetted with a solution of detergent and water. If your supplier offers this option, take it. It makes things much easier, but in any case, follow the manufacturer's directions very closely.

Begin by lifting up the sandwich on its hinge and taping it in the raised position. If you've cut to form an arc, each section will have to be taped. If the lettering is straight, imitate the arc by cutting the sandwich into several smaller, manageable sections (individual letters will be easiest) and taping up each one. In either case, make sure the tape hinge stays firmly in place to preserve alignment.

Starting at one end, remove the protective sheet from each letter or section. Lower the letter and overlay back in place, using a squeegee to apply pressure to the overlay starting from the hinge and working away from it, pushing any trapped air ahead of the vinyl as you go. It may take several strokes of the squeegee to ensure that air bubbles are worked out. Repeat this for each letter or section, working your way across the surface. Allow the completed application to set according to the manufacturer's directions before removing the overlay and inspecting the results. Any air bubbles that remain can be pricked with a pin and carefully squeegeed flat.

This is definitely a situation where a bit of planning and a thoughtful, measured approach will go a long way towards a first-class outcome. At the very least, it will ensure that people aren't staring at your stern for the wrong reasons.

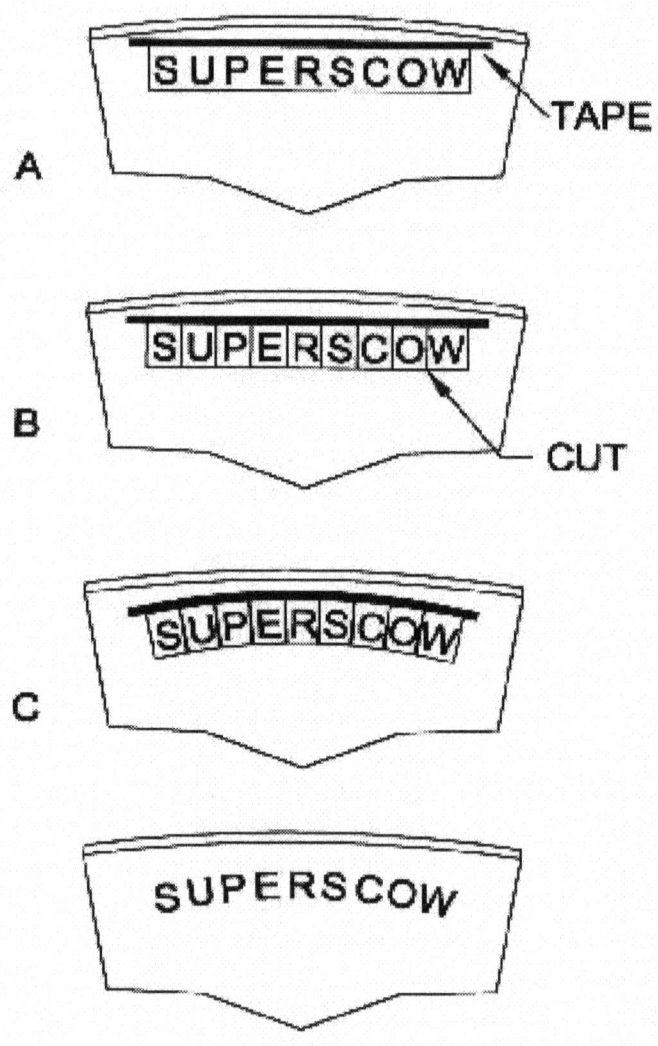

Figure 27-1
Applying vinyl lettering.

Chapter Twenty-Eight
Fender Addenda

Fenders are handy for some boat owners and an absolute necessity for others. I fall in the latter category. The townhouse development where I live doesn't allow storage of boats or trailers, so I've always kept my boats in a slip on the river. Even without the wind, the wakes of passing boats or changing tides, the river is always on the move, so sturdy fenders are required to prevent damage. I equipped my first boat with inexpensive inflatable fenders that did a remarkably good job for the four years.

When the new, larger boat arrived, I splurged for a set of fenders with horizontal ribs. They were more expensive than the plain, slick kind, but they were heavier, sturdier and looked like they'd take more of a beating.

Toward the end of the first season, I noticed some marks on the hull in the shape of an arc where the fenders swung back and forth, but I figured the dealer had simply done a poor job of waxing the new boat and that a good polish would take care of them. You can imagine my dismay when I discovered the marks were actually grooves worn into the gel-coat by those sturdy fender ribs.

Even though the fenders were properly inflated, much of the load of the boat being pushed against the fender was concentrated at the very small pressure points provided by the ribs. (See Figure 1.) The result was abrasion severe enough to damage the hull.

I've since replaced the ribbed fenders with the plain, low-tech slick variety, although I assume that fenders with subtle vertical ribs would have been an improvement too. The new fenders' smooth contour spreads out the load over a very wide area, reducing the pressure-per-square-inch to insignificance and thus do a better job. They aren't very sexy, but neither are worn spots on the topsides.

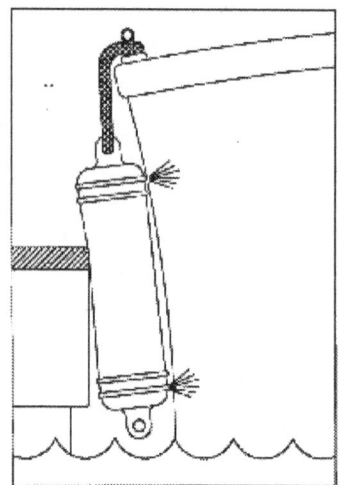 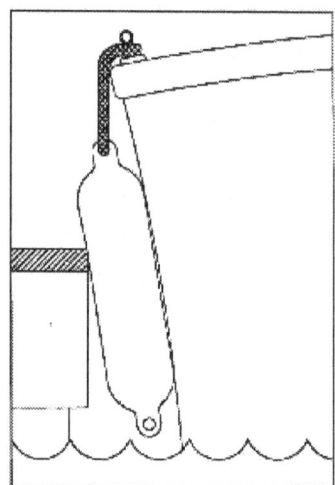

Figure 28-1
Comparison of the action of ribbed and smooth fenders.

Securing fenders can be a problem, too; it is a rare boat with cleats everywhere you need them. Perhaps it's a money issue. Manufacturers always look for ways to cut costs, although it's hard to imagine that the added cost of a pair of well-placed cleats would be a show-stopper. Builders of trailer boats who have convinced themselves that theirs will never see a dock may have decided attachment points are unnecessary. Whatever the reason, there's rarely a fender cleat where you need it most, right where the bow broadens to nearly beam width.

This area is also a good place to consider a different fender type. Because of flare or overhang, it can make sense to consider a ball-shape fender in place of the traditional oblong. The added diameter does a better job of taking up the space between the hull and the dock (See Figure 2), resulting in more stable positioning of the boat. The drawback is that it makes the fenders more difficult to stow, but the shape provides much better protection.

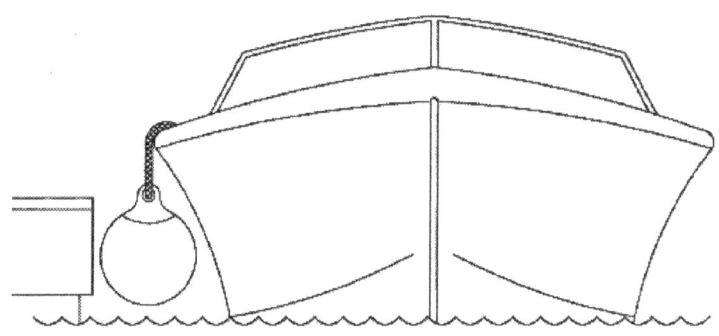

Figure 28-2
A ball fender fills the gap

The most obvious remedy is to install cleats where you need them. For owners hesitant to drill holes in their boats, there are numerous plastic clips, ties, hoops and other devices for hanging fenders from rails, handles or windshields. When I had to decide how to mount the forward fenders on my new boat, I chose cleats where needed rather than rely on a plastic clip.

Because of the conditions at my dock, I needed the security of metal cleats.

My plan was to install four-inch cleats with long #10 sheet-metal screws to attach them to the deck. Since they would only be exposed to the stress of the fender, they wouldn't need backing plates, and their small size would discourage unfamiliar dock-hands from trying to tie a line to them. But first I thought I'd rig a fender temporarily by tying it to a rail stanchion and use it for a while to see if I'd chosen the best location. The problem was that neither Pat, my First Mate, nor I is a potential winner in a knot-tying contest. Our knots usually end up looking like a ball of twine that the cat has been playing with, and they seem to unravel just as quickly. I needed a better solution for my temporary fender rig.

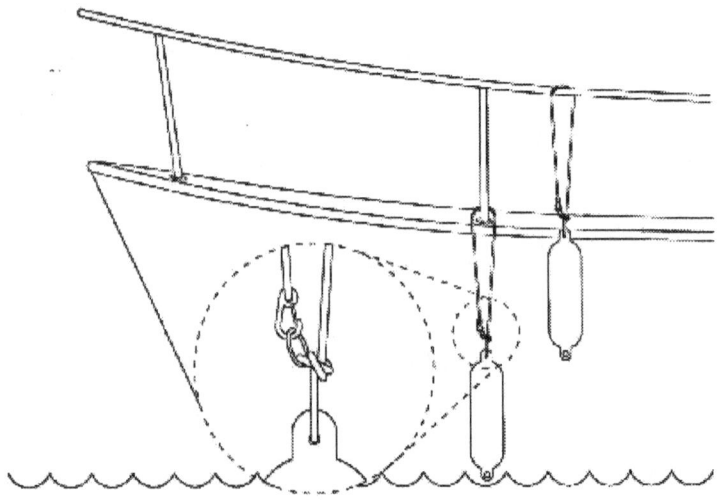

Figure 28-3
A quick-connect fender line.

I began by binding a stainless-steel O-ring into the knot that attaches the line to the fender. Then I attached a snap-shackle to the bitter end (a snap or carabiner would have done as well). Including the ring, all are readily available at marine suppliers. The set-up allowed the First Mate to rig for docking by looping the fender line around a rail stanchion, clipping the snap-shackle to the ring and dropping the fender overboard. (See Figure 3.) I made the line long enough so the fender is normally suspended just above the waterline. It worked.

Actually, it worked too well. It was so easy to use that First Mate wanted nothing to do with additional cleats. "Why should I fool around with tying and readjusting a line to a cleat when I can just snap this together and toss it overboard", she asked, "and it's always exactly the right height!" I decided she was right. Not only was it easier to use, it was more secure than tying to a cleat and neater, too — no loose ends flapping in the breeze. For special situations like a high dock, the fender can be raised by taking a few turns around the stanchion. For rafting up with another boat, it can be suspended from the rail. And the fact that all the hardware is located right at the fender's attachment loop keeps it from chafing the boat's topsides.

Does this put the manufacturers of all those nifty clips out of business? Not at all. For boats without rails or stanchions in the right place, or where the fender must be suspended from the windshield frame or other structure, clips and similar devices are a workable solution. But don't waste your time trying to talk the First Mate out of her fender suspenders.

Modern Boatworks -- By David S. Yetman

Chapter Twenty-Nine
Propeller Resurrection

Someone once said, "The only boaters who haven't dinged a propeller are those who don't leave the dock." Whoever it was must have been from New England, knowing full well that it's boating among the rocks. Rocks are tough on props and so ubiquitous that their damage is usually written off. Prudent skippers hesitate to leave the dock without a spare prop or two.

My first boat, a brand new 22-footer, had exactly 36 minutes on it when I mangled the prop by introducing it to a five-ton rock at eight knots. Embarrassed, mad and fearful of what I'd done, I limped back to the marina and hauled the boat out onto its trailer. While dejectedly staring at the black-and-silver cauliflower that had been my prop and pondering its replacement, the marina manager came over and suggested I send it out for repair. I was surprised that something so obviously damaged could even be a candidate for repair but decided to check it out.

To get a first-hand look at how such resurrections are accomplished, I visited the local propeller shop, where the manager graciously consented to give me the full tour and demonstrate the wizardry.

The process begins with triage, separating the repairable from the hopeless. From a technical perspective, very few props are beyond repair. An intact hub with little left of the blades but stubs can be reconstructed, but the time consumed would drive the cost to exceed the price of a new prop. At the height of the boating season, when the workload can be hundreds of props per week, there's no time to waste on hopeless cases. Fortunately, much of the typical workload involves props with minor nicks and bends, defects that appear insignificant but can still affect efficiency.

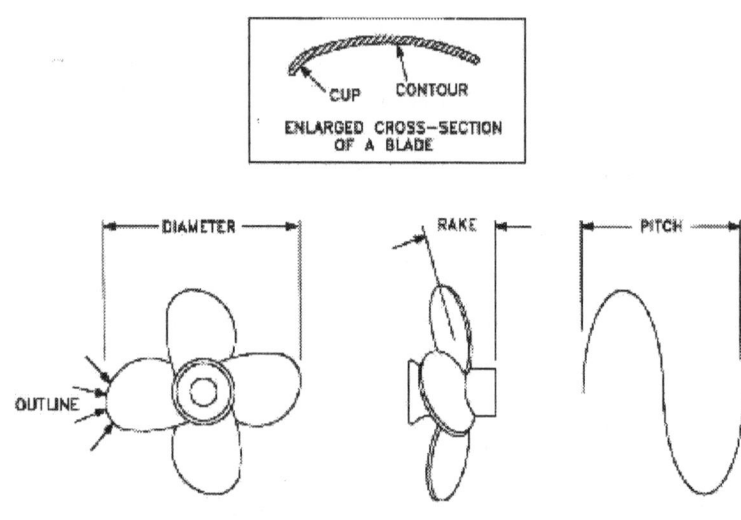

Figure 29-1
Propeller properties.

Repairing propellers is not a pretty, prissy business. It's done by a team of hard-working craftsmen imposing their will on recalcitrant metal with tools and methods as far from subtle as you can get. Their abundant skills weren't honed at Harvard but rather learned the hard way in long, sweaty apprenticeships. They are immensely proud of their craft, more art than science and closer to blacksmithing than high-tech. The tools are a hold-over from the smithy as well - heat, hammers, anvils and long levers to assist in bending metal back into shape. The basic repair process is the same for all of the most common prop materials — aluminum, bronze, nibral and stainless steel.

Although I was aware of the brutish nature of the task, I was still unprepared for the hazy bedlam of the shop floor: the hellish clang of hammers on bronze, the whine of grinding wheels and the constant whoosh of exhaust systems straining to control the dust and detritus.

Figure 29-2
Reshaping the blade of a damaged prop over an anvil.

In one corner of the shop, the "patients" were stacked on poles to await their turn at rehabilitation. When its time arrives, each prop will be mounted on the vertical spindle of a repair station that looks much like an automotive tire-repair stand. There, whatever remains of its blades will be hammered back into rough shape over a removable steel anvil attached to the station platform. The anvil has to be removable because every prop from every manufacturer has to have its own anvil shape. For example, if a manufacturer offered props in nine diameters and eight different pitches, that means that 72 different anvils have to be available in order to service that line completely. In addition to variations in diameter and pitch, they must also accommodate different rakes, the angle at which the blades lean aft.

Figure 29-3
Grinding excess weld material off a repaired propeller.

Once the blades have been roughly straightened, their edges are compared to a scribed outline on the anvil to determine how much metal has to be added to bring it back to its original size and shape. This information is drawn and written on each blade before it's sent to the welding station, where missing metal is replaced by laboriously welding multiple beads along the edges. No filler pieces are welded; all of the new metal is deposited by welding. Excess metal is then ground off before the prop goes back to the anvil for final shaping of the outline and contours.

That's easily said, but even the most thorough description of the process would fail to convey the hundreds of subtleties involved. Differences for dual-prop drives, specialty props, tricks to keep props from singing or cavitating and countless other bits of knowledge are essential parts of the craft. These are the details that make a three-knot difference or, in extreme cases, the difference between a prop that works and one that doesn't.

After being sanded smooth at a buffing station, the prop will be balanced, have its cup (a subtle flip at the trailing edge) hammered back in, then smoothed once more before being repainted if it's aluminum or polished if it's bronze or nibral. The result is a propeller nearly indistinguishable from a new one in strength, performance and appearance.

The service that propeller shops provide is a valuable one, but it doesn't alleviate the pain and embarrassment that come with messing up your prop. And it's hard to have confidence in the process unless you've benefited from it. I remember being so doubtful about the results of having that first prop rebuilt that I bought a brand-new one while I was waiting for it to be returned. To my amazement, the rebuild ran smoother than it did when it was new. The new one ended up as my spare, but not for long. I totally destroyed the rebuilt one just six weeks later.

A Mount for Your Spare Prop

Prudent skippers carry spare props for inevitable emergencies, but because they're an odd shape they're difficult to stow. They're also subject to damage if left to rattle around in the bilge or stowed under a heavy object.

One method is to store the prop in a safe location on an accessory mount. While prop mounts are available commercially, (Mercury offers a nice one), it's also easy to make one from a railing-stanchion base fitting and a length of metal tubing or a stout hardwood dowel. (See Figure 4.) It can be mounted to any sturdy, out-of-the-way surface, including bulkheads, stringers or the wall of a lazarette. Rail base fittings are available at most marine stores. They come in rectangular or round shapes (the rectangular has four mounting holes, not three), are available in sizes to accept 7/8" and 1" tubing and made from either stainless steel or an aluminum - magnesium - zinc alloy. Use the far-stronger stainless one unless your prop is a featherweight.

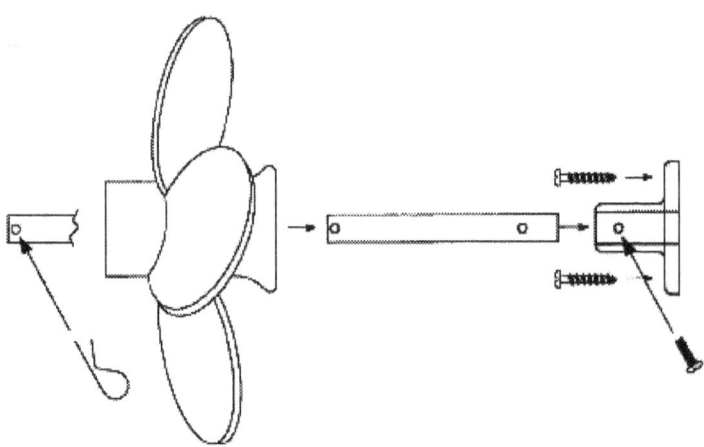

Figure 29-4
Spare propeller mount.

Modern Boatworks -- By David S. Yetman

Drill a hole in the tubing or dowel to match the one(s) in the sidewall of the base. Any setscrews supplied should be discarded in favor of a screw that goes through at least one wall of the tube (two is better) or deeply into the dowel. Drill another hole in the opposite end for a horseshoe clip or cotter pin to keep the prop in place. For outboard or I/O props, placing them on the peg face-first will make the horseshoe clip easier to access. If you have space, cover the tube with a length of rubber hose or plastic sleeving to protect the prop's internal splines or keyway.

Modern Boatworks -- *By David S. Yetman*

Chapter Thirty
Choosing the Correct Oil

Motor oil is the lifeblood of our boats' motors, which have been quietly reinvented over the last generation or so. Modern internal-combustion engines produce more clean power and outlast anything available to our fathers, regardless of price. This highly successful evolution would not have been possible without parallel advances in metallurgy and lubricant technology, most of which have remained transparent to the users.

That transparency may not be in our best interests. Stranded at the dock one recent windy day, I found myself thinking about the ancient Nash Ambassador sedan that a girlfriend's father sold me many years ago. In retrospect, I think it was more an act of revenge than commerce because the beast consumed motor oil at a rate I couldn't afford to support. But during its final days I still had to find a way to feed its prodigious appetite, so I resorted to collecting gallons of used motor oil from several service stations. The majority of the sediment and visible contaminants would settle to the bottom of the can after a few days, allowing me to siphon off the upper two-thirds of the clarified liquid for use in the car. In the ultimate act of technical indifference, I never gave a thought to the grade, viscosity, service rating or origins of the lubricant. I cared only about cost and availability: zero and easy, respectively.

My inattention to such details carried through to later years when I began to race sports cars as an amateur. By then I was no longer forced to recycle others' oil, but my attitude was still, "Oil is oil. Why get bogged down in the details?" That changed when I became infatuated with the technical elegance and intricacies of Japanese motorcycle engines. I thought any machine that ran at 11,000 rpm needed all the support it could get, so I started paying attention to the manufacturer's oil recommendations.

I really sat up and took notice when I became the owner of a new diesel powered boat. Reading the engine manual, I was struck by a statement in which the manufacturer said that if its recommended oil wasn't available and had to be replaced with next-lower grade, the time between oil changes had to be cut in half. In other words, one type of oil would protect my new engine twice as long as a perfectly good oil of the wrong grade. That made me a believer. I immediately fired off a request to the American Petroleum Institute (API) for all the information they could supply to me.

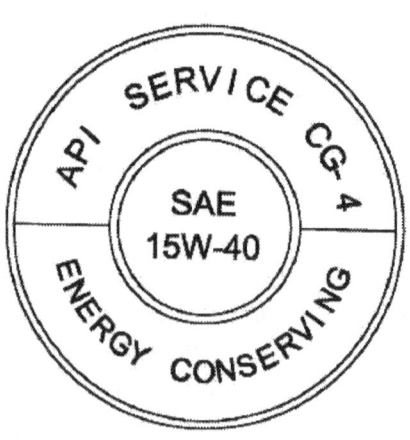

Figure 30-1
The API symbol.

API SERVICE CATEGORIES	
GASOLINE ENGINES	DIESEL ENGINES
SA - Obsolete	CA - Obsolete. For light duty engines (1940s and 1950s)
SB - Obsolete	CB - Obsolete. For moderate duty engines (1949 to 1960)
SC - Obsolete. For 1967 and older engines	CC - Obsolete. For engines introduced in 1961
SD - Obsolete. For 1971 and older engines	CD - Obsolete. Introduced in 1955 for certain naturally aspirated and turbocharged engines
SE - Obsolete. For 1979 and older engines	CD-II - Obsolete. Introduced in 1987 for two- stroke cycle engines
SF - Obsolete. For 1988 and older engines	CE - Obsolete. For high-speed, four-stroke cycle, naturally aspirated and turbocharged engines. Can be used in place of CC and CD oils
SG - Obsolete. For 1993 and older engines	CF-4 - Current. Introduced in 1990 for high-speed, four-stroke cycle, naturally aspirated and turbocharged engines. Can be used in place of CE oils
SH - Current. Introduced 1993. Discontinued after 1997 except when used in combination with some C categories.	CF - Current. Introduced in 1994 for off-road, indirect-injected and other diesel engines including those using fuel with over 0.5% weight sulfur. Can be used in place of CD oils
SJ - Current. Introduced 1996. For all engines currently in use.	CF-2 - Current. Introduced in 1994 for severe- duty, two-stroke cycle engines. Can be used in place of CD-II oils
Note: Each gasoline category above exceeds the performance properties of all the previous categories and can be used in place of the lower one.	CG-4 - Current. Introduced in 1995 for severe duty, four-stroke cycle engines using fuel with less than 0.5% weight sulfur. Can be used in place of CD, CE and CF-4 oils

Figure 30-2
API Service Category Chart.

Motor oil for internal combustion engines is described in three ways: by type (natural mineral oil, synthetic or a blend of the two); by viscosity (how well it flows at specific temperatures), and by service classification (the ability to provide protection under specific operating conditions). Although the last two are independent, both are necessary to define an oil's performance characteristics and can be applied to either natural or synthetic lubricants.

A large majority of the motor oil is natural, refined and modified with additives to meet specific performance requirements. Interestingly, only two quarts of each 42- gallon barrel of crude oil ends up as lubricating oil; the balance ends up mainly as gasoline and fuel oil. Synthetic lubricants, originally developed for severe-service applications such as jet engines, are becoming more widely available, often in a natural/synthetic blend that takes advantage of the qualities of both.

Viscosity is classified under a standard set by the Society of Automotive Engineers (SAE), which assigns numbers from SAE 0 to SAE 60 to motor oils (60 being the most viscous). A "W" designation such as SAE 10W indicates that the oil has been formulated to flow easily during low-temperature winter use. Designations with no W such as SAE 30 must meet viscosity specifications at high-temperature and are tested at 212_F (100C). The designation for a multi-grade oil such as SAE 10W-40 indicates it will perform well under cold conditions but also meet viscosity requirements at the other end of its temperature range.

It's important to remember the SAE designation specifies viscosity only and is independent from API service classifications. These are established under the Engine Oil Licensing and Certification System (EOLCS) developed in conjunction with international engine and vehicle manufacturers and their trade associations. According to the API, the system enables "motor oils to be defined and selected on the basis of their performance characteristics and the type of service for which they were intended." It allows the engine manufacturer to specify an oil that will provide the appropriate level of protection and gives consumers confidence that they are purchasing exactly what the manufacturer specified. The API service classification and the SAE viscosity of oil are shown on a donut-shaped marking called the API Service Symbol on the oil container (See Figure 1).

The EOLCS was designed to be a dynamic system that would accommodate changing requirements as technologies advanced and improved fuels became available. The increasing pace of change is evident in the API Service Category Chart (Figure 2.). Where older classifications remained current for nearly a decade, later ones are often superseded in two or three years. The advent of turbochargers, superchargers, lean-burning motors and much higher-performance engines have placed an escalating burden on motor oils. Modern lubricants are regularly enhanced with additives such as detergents, viscosity improvers, anti-wear agents and other ingredients which inhibit corrosion, oxidation and foaming.

Oil selection for owners of gasoline engines is relatively straightforward because there are a very small number of current "S" classifications, each useable in place of any previous classification. The "C" classifications for diesel engines are more complex because of the different requirements of two- and four-stroke engines (normally aspirated) versus turbocharged engines and recent changes in sulfur content of diesel fuels mandated by EPA guidelines. Later classifications may not be appropriate replacements for earlier ones, so careful selection is important. But the complexity isn't a stumbling block because matching the manufacturer's recommended oil classification and adhering to their oil and filter-change interval assures the protection they've specified.

Chapter Thirty-One
Oil and Analysis

Your doctor uses blood analysis as a primary tool to evaluate your condition and diagnose what ails you. Boat owners who want to monitor the condition of their engines have access to similar diagnostic wizardry in the form of oil analysis.

Where blood analysis is an extension of hematology, oil analysis is a part of the science of tribology, the study of lubrication, friction and wear. Oil analysis is quick, easy and so inexpensive that it should be an integral part of every owner's long- term maintenance plan. The analysis of a few ounces of used oil will provide a wealth of information about is condition and, by extension, the engine's condition as well. Among the more than 20 tests commonly done, those to detect viscosity changes, dilution by fuel, the presence of contaminants such as water, antifreeze and dirt and the amount of suspended metallic debris produced by wear provide the most immediate value.

The information from these tests can have implications far beyond its face value. The condition of the oil at a given point are valuable feedback about the way the engine is used, the type of oil it requires and other internal conditions, including abnormal wear and impending failure. If the oil has lost its original viscosity, it may indicate the need for an improved grade. The presence of fuel may indicate a problem in the fuel system, causing an excessively rich mixture or fuel that isn't being burned completely. Contamination by water or antifreeze can indicate leaking seals, or worse, a crack in an engine casting. A concentration of non-ferrous metals such as tin or lead (components of babbitt material) may warn of impending bearing failure. Excessive soot deposits may be the result of piston-ring blow-by. The presence of elevated levels of metallic particles is a sure sign of excess wear.

A single analysis will provide a good snapshot of an engine's condition, but the real value can only be realized if the analysis is part of a regularly scheduled series of evaluations. This is especially true of engines such as diesels that really put their lubricants to the test, yet are expected to provide service over an extended lifetime.

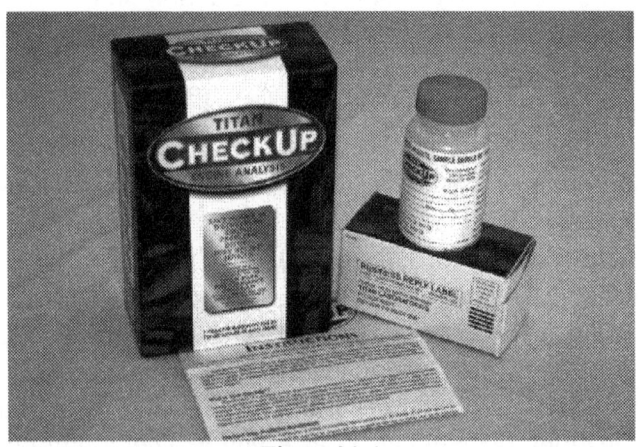

Figure 31-1
A single-use oil analysis kit.

Regular analysis is no less important for boats that don't get much use. Those that don't get up to full operating temperature can build up condensation; corrosive elements can form in the oil and seals can dry out and fail. The results of regular oil analysis provide a running history of an engine's condition so that trends can be spotted and corrective measures taken before a problem ends up causing a catastrophic failure.

Analysis records as part of an organized maintenance program will also add resale value to the boat when it's time to move up. Oil analysis is available through many oil distributors, engine manufacturers and dealers and directly from laboratories. For example, Caterpillar has a highly organized program offered through its dealers.

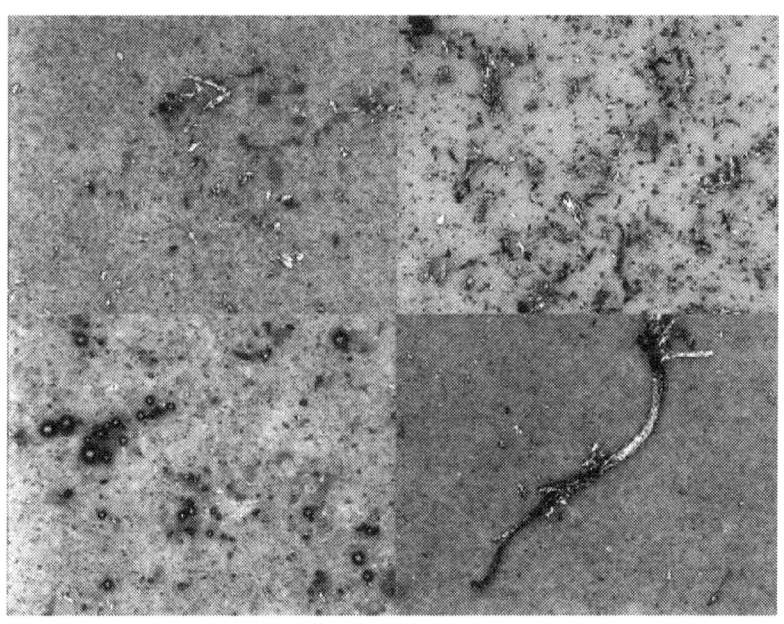

Figure 31-2
Courtesy of Butler Machinery Company
Highly magnified views of metallic wear particles detected in oil during analysis.

Most laboratories offer a standard set of tests for a fixed fee that can range from $12 to more than $60, depending on the number of tests performed. Most will provide by mail the user with a sampling kit and complete instructions. If some potentially critical observation results, some labs will also call the customer rather than waiting for the mail to deliver the warning. In some cases, the lab may also suggest you submit a sample of new oil of the type you normally use so it can establish a base line for comparison. You can find local labs under "Laboratories, Testing" in the phone book or by doing an Internet search on "oil analysis."

Figure 31-3
Courtesy of National Tribology Services
Laboratory technicians using spectrometers to analyze oil samples.

Obtaining the sample is straightforward, but like a hematologist drawing blood, some precautions are necessary to prevent contamination of the sample and misleading results. A clean container is a must. Most labs recommend the oil sample be siphoned or pumped from an engine that's been running long enough to reach its normal operating temperature. Engines with the benefit of continuing analysis are often fitted with an inexpensive sampling valve so oil can be drawn quickly and easily. If this isn't practical and the sample must be obtained from drained oil, it should be taken after about half of the engine's oil has been drained to avoid picking up a concentration of contaminants in the bottom of the sump. The sample should not be taken from a drain pan or container used for other purposes, as it may contain elements unconnected with the engine's condition.

Oil analysis is widely used by operators of long-haul trucks, off-road equipment and heavy machinery, but it isn't restricted to diesel engines. And there are inexpensive tests available for cooling systems, too. The information these tests can provide makes them one of the most important and cost-effective maintenance tools you can employ.

OIL SAMPLE TESTING

Caterpillar's scheduled oil sampling analysis program encourages long-term, regularly scheduled sampling as part of an overall preventive-maintenance plan. Cat offers a complete sampling kit which includes a pump and tubing for sampling through a dipstick tube, an attachment for drawing from a permanently installed sample valve, prepaid mailers for oil and coolant analysis, instructions and program information. Best of all, you don't need a Caterpillar engine to make use of the program.

Modern Boatworks -- By David S. Yetman

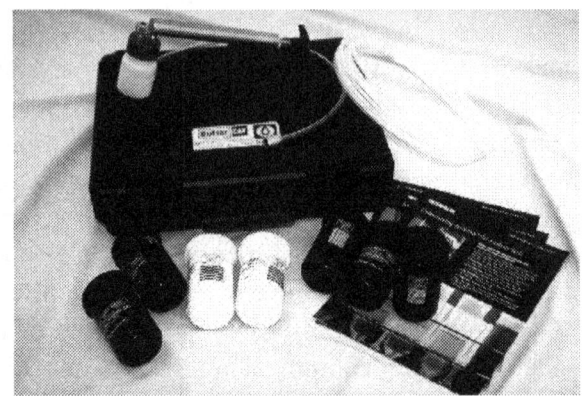

Figure 31-4
Caterpillar's S-O-S analysis program kit.

Chapter Thirty-Two
Clean & Easy Oil Changes

It would be nice if choosing the correct oil and monitoring its condition were the only aspects of engine lubrication, but there's more to it than that. Engine oil degrades and is contaminated during use, so has to be drained and replaced on a regular basis.

Handling oil presents some unique opportunities to create problems, not the least of which are environmental concerns associated with leakage and spills. Changing the oil filter on an I/O or inboard not equipped with a remote-mounted filter is a good example. It can be nearly impossible to do without spilling some oil. Even the apparent convenience of a remote filter is no guarantee of spill-free changes. Considering the mess it causes and the penalties for discharging even small amounts of pollutants, it makes great sense to exert the extra effort that it takes to do it right.

The location of the oil filter on my first boat was nearly inaccessible to a normally formed human being. My long arms would just barely allow me to get a wrench on the filter, but very often I was unable to prevent the filter and its load of dirty oil from dropping into the bilge. After trying several solutions and suffering some spectacular failures, I came up with a solution that worked perfectly. I constructed a frame as shown in Figure 1 by twisting together some coat-hanger wire, a frame with a short leg that hooked over the hull stringer and a longer leg resting in the bilge. I stretched a small plastic bag over the frame as shown in Figure 1 and secured it with just enough bits of tape to hold it in place while I wrestled it into position under the oil filter as shown in Figure 1. Then I unscrewed the filter and let it drop into the bag, which also caught any oil overflow. When the excess oil had drained completely, I separated the bag from the frame while it was still in the bilge, cinched it up and carefully removed it.

In practice, I found it was best to use a wrench to loosen the filter (without breaking the seal) before putting the bag in place. I also placed a rag or some paper towels in the bottom of the bag as a cushion to prevent the filter from causing a puncture when it dropped. While this may sound like a lot of trouble, it's easier than cleaning the bilge and cheaper than paying fines.

I was sure I'd put those problems behind me when I bought my second boat, a single-screw diesel whose oil filter was mounted high and near the front of the engine. Unfortunately, the engine was mated to a V-drive, so it sat backward in the engine box with the oil filter snugly nestled into a corner under the hinged engine cover. I could reach it, but there was no way to get a standard filter wrench on it. Although I managed to modify an automotive filter wrench so I could loosen the old filter, I couldn't position the wrench so I could tighten the new one.

I solved the problem by installing the new filter as tightly as possible by hand, then wrapping a piece of small braided line around the filter for two loops in the fashion of a clove hitch. (See Figure 2.) While maintaining considerable tension on the "free" end of the line, I was able to pull on the other end with sufficient force to rotate the filter the final 3/4 turn needed to seal properly. The rope "wrench" can be used on any spin-on filter cartridge. Because it's not very efficient, it limits the amount of torque that can be applied to the filter, but this is a hidden benefit. Since the filter can't be over-tightened, the rope wrench can be used to remove it as well.

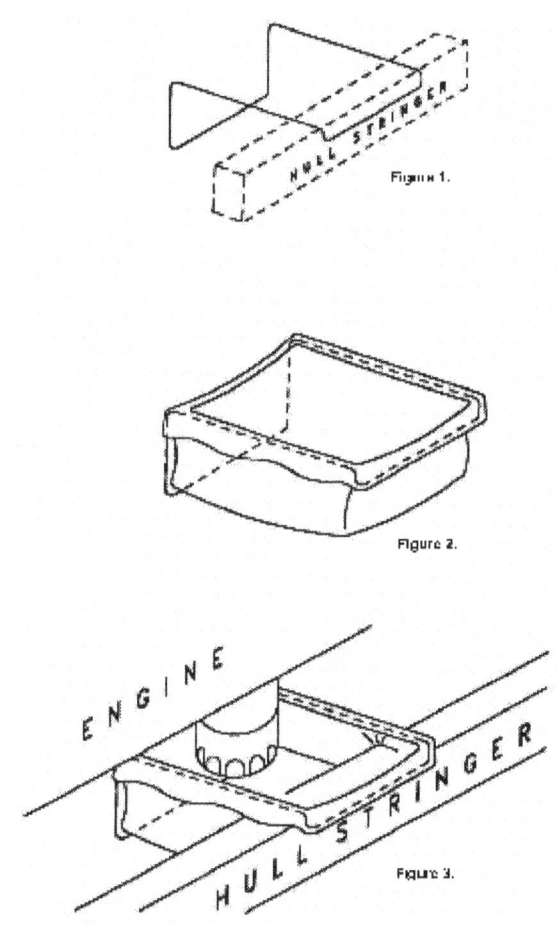

Building a catch-basin for oil and filter.

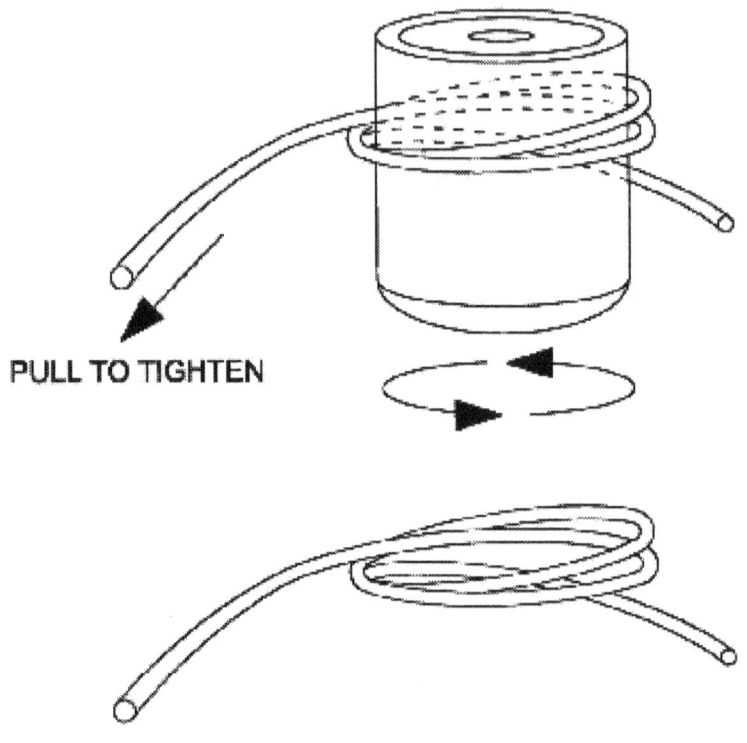

Figure 32-2
A filter "wrench" for tight spots.

Having spent so much time and effort to keep oil out of the bilge, I was really frustrated when the engine developed an oil leak, only detectable by an ugly slick. After searching unsuccessfully for the source for several weeks, I devised a method to find its general location and narrow the search.

I cut a square section out of an old bed sheet about as long as the engine and attached a four-foot length of string to each of its corners. Then, with the help of another person, I positioned the cloth under the engine (careful to keep it out of the bilge) and tied the strings to various points to keep it suspended. After checking to see that the sling wasn't in contact with any moving parts, we took a short cruise to warm up the engine, then carefully removed the sling. Sure enough, it had a nice, dark oil spot just below an oil-line fitting hidden behind the fuel-metering pump and a large raw-water intake line. With the aid of a mirror and an extension light, I was able to apply a couple of turns of a wrench to cure the problem.

Unfortunately, even fastidious attention and careful maintenance will not guarantee an oil-free bilge, so it's a good idea to keep an oil-absorbent sock or two in the bilge. Attaching them with a line to some point above the water level will keep them in place and make them easier to retrieve later. All used filters and oil-soaked clean-up materials should be disposed of in a responsible manner.

Modern Boatworks -- By David S. Yetman

Chapter Thirty-Three
Hanging by a Thread

Maintenance is a fact of life, much of it involving screws, nuts and bolts. Even the simplest runabout suffers no shortage of bits and pieces to loosen up and fall off or seize up, steadfastly resisting any effort to remove them. The bad news is that the situation is unlikely to change.

Other than adhesives or rivets, screws and bolts are the most efficient and reliable way to attach things to each other. Yet the combination of metal and moisture, especially salt water, will continue to cause problems in the form of rust and corrosion.

The good news is that many of the difficulties can be prevented or corrected by using the right fasteners and installing them properly. Whether you're adding an accessory, making repairs or restoring a boat from the keel up, basic knowledge about threaded fasteners can be one of your most useful tools.

Types of Hardware

Screws and bolts literally could fill a book. *Machinery's Handbook* lists more than a dozen basic types of threaded fasteners, over 100 different thread sizes, scores of head types and many different materials, adding up to thousands of choices. Thankfully, we need consider just a few of the most common types and sizes.

In nearly all instances, stainless steel should be the material of choice. Figure 1 shows five common types.

Wood screws are used solely where wood is the host material. They are the original self-tapping screw, since they can often be inserted with no more preparation than a small starter hole. To use them in a hardwood such as teak, however, requires a pilot hole of the correct size to facilitate entry and to avoid splitting the host material. They are kept in place by friction alone.

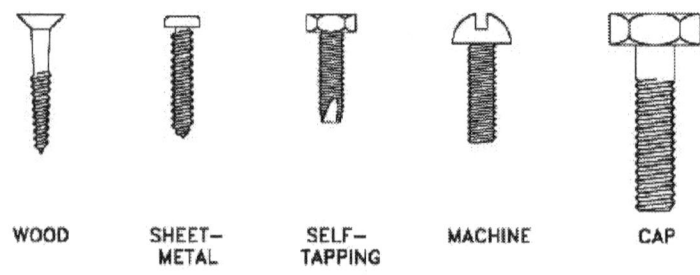

Figure 33-1
Profiles of common screw types.

Sheet-metal screws were originally designed to be used where the host material is a thin metal sheet, but their application has been greatly expanded so that modern varieties are used in almost any non-metallic host material, including wood. They are ubiquitous and used to mount everything from accessories to interior upholstery and joinery. In most materials, they require a pilot hole, and in hard materials such as fiberglass, the size of the hole is critical. If it's too small, the screw may be difficult to install and the host material may be damaged if the screw is forced in. Making the pilot hole too large will result in a loss of holding power.

Self-tapping screws are designed to be used in hard materials, where the benefits of fairly well-formed threads such as increased holding power or ease of entry are required. The screw will have slots or flats in its first few threads that result in sharp cutting edges that form threads on the way into the host material. Widely used in the appliance industry, they are rarely seen in boats.

Machine screws are designed to be used in conjunction with matching nuts or in a relatively hard host material tapped with matching internal threads. The term is usually used for screws designed to be used with a screwdriver or similar hand tool and whose diameter is described by a gauge number (e.g., #8) rather than a fraction such as 1/4". (That distinction doesn't apply to metric screws because they're dimensioned in millimeters.) Because of their need to be precisely matched to components that will accept them, the threads of machine screws are manufactured to meet very exacting standards. They're identified by a two-part designation such as 6-32 or 10-24; the first part is the nominal diameter of the screw; the second is the number of threads per inch of length.

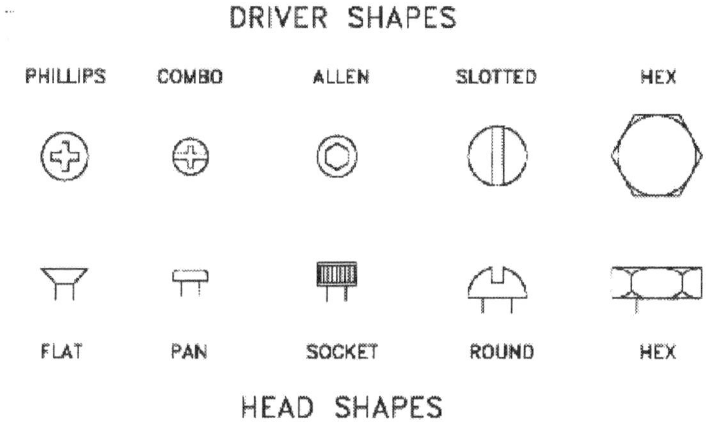

DRIVER SHAPES

PHILLIPS COMBO ALLEN SLOTTED HEX

FLAT PAN SOCKET ROUND HEX

HEAD SHAPES

Figure 33-2
Common screw head and driver shapes.

Bolts and cap screws are larger-diameter machine screws designed to be used with wrenches that permit them to be tightened to the higher degree that their heavier loads require. They have all the features and standardization of machine screws, except that their diameter is usually specified as a fraction of an inch such as 1/4-20 or 1/2-13.

No discussion would be complete without a brief review of head shapes and the different types of drivers. There are a large number of special-purpose drivers, such as the square- and star-shape adopted by specific industries but aren't usually seen in boats. (Figure 2 shows some of the most common types.) Most screws are available in almost any combination of head and drive types, but cap screws and bolts tend to be limited to socket- and hex-head configurations only.

Nuts

While there are almost as many types of nuts as there are screws, only a few are common. Figure 3 shows three: the ubiquitous hex-nut, castle-nut and elastic stop-nut. The latter two are locking nuts that eliminate the need for lock washers.

There are two types of castle nuts. One provides enough space between the "parapets" to allow a cotter pin to be inserted through a hole in the bolt. The other is a jam nut; its parapets are bent slightly in so that they are a jam-fit on the screw, using metal-to-metal friction to prevent it from loosening. This is very effective but can be a problem if the nut needs to be removed. The extreme friction can damage the screw threads and even cause the nut to seize to the screw or bolt. The elastic stop-nut also uses friction to do its job but relies on the pressure from a nylon insert (much kinder to the threads) to provide grip. While they're a far more expensive solution, elastic stop-nuts in a variety of sizes are widely used in aircraft and electronics or anywhere that a loose nut could result in damage, failure or a safety hazard. Attaching outdrive units is a common marine use.

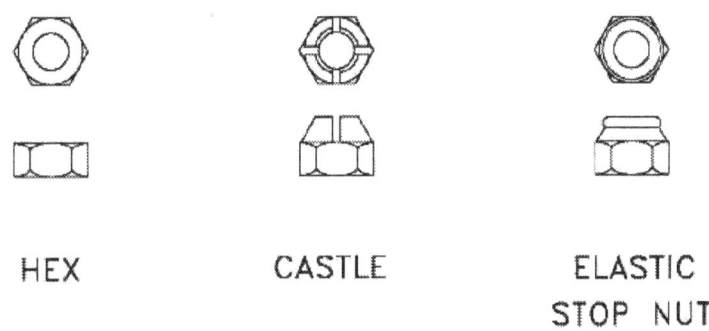

Figure 33-3
Various nut styles.

Washers

Figure 4 shows the four main washer types. The split-lock is the most common and is usually used in heavy-duty applications. Its main drawback is that it has only one gripping edge per side. Star washers, whether internally or externally serrated, have many more gripping edges but may be less effective in high-load situations because they're made from thinner stock. Flat washers, which are used to protect finishes and spread loads, are available in three different outside diameters for each screw diameter, small pattern washers for tight spaces, standard diameter and fender washers for situations where the load must be spread out over a larger area. As their name implies, fender washers were originally used to hold fenders to car bodies without tearing through the relatively thin sheet metal of the fender.

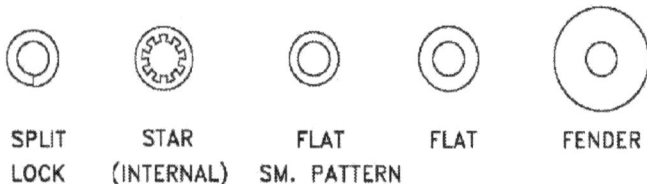

| SPLIT LOCK | STAR (INTERNAL) | FLAT SM. PATTERN | FLAT | FENDER |

Figure 33-4
Outlines of washer types.

Matching the Fastener to the Job

The basic rule is quite simple: in any application where access will permit, use a machine screw, nut and appropriate washers. It's the strongest and most reliable way to attach one thing to another and still be able to separate them when necessary. It's especially true for installing high-stress accessories such as cleats, bitts or chain plates where the use of a backing plate may be essential in distributing loads placed on the screws or bolts. The material of choice stainless steel for its strength and durability.

Unfortunately, most situations don't permit the best solutions, but in many instances an alternate method will work almost as well if done properly. Sheet-metal screws are adequate for mounting many accessories where access to the rear of the panel isn't available. If the accessory's mounting flanges are thin or made from a soft material, a screw with a large-diameter head will provide holding power with less chance of damage or failure. A flat washer under the head can provide extra protection.

Use flathead screws in situations where a protruding head would be a problem, but be careful not to overtighten them. The conical shape of the heads' underside can result in outward pressure if overtightened, causing material such as fiberglass to crack and fail eventually.

Ease of Installation

Installing a screw for the first time is usually only difficult if it's done wrong. If a wood screw or sheet-metal screw is resisting your best efforts, it's probably because the screw is too long, the pilot hole is too small (or non-existent), or the wrong type of screw is being used. If the hole isn't a clearance hole (larger than the diameter of the screw), this can also add to the problem. In any of these cases, you face the risk of breaking off the screw or damaging the host material.

Sheet-metal screws are not designed to be used in thick or hard metals, even with the proper-size pilot hole. Use a self-tapping screw or, better still, tap the hole and use a machine screw. There are times when even the right screw going into a properly sized pilot hole will still present a problem. In this case, a lubricant can ease the entry and prevent damage, but be very careful about choosing the lubricant. I once read an article where the author suggested using Teflon grease to ease the entry of a sheet-metal screw into stainless-steel tubing. I can think of no better way to ensure that a screw will loosen up than to coat it with a permanently slippery substance like Teflon. A much better solution would have been to use self-tapping screws.

My favorite lubricant, especially for working in fiberglass, is silicone. It lubricates the entry of the screw, seals the exposed edges of the fiberglass and then cures to a rubber-like consistency that not only helps lock the screw in place but seals the hole as well.

Keeping Them Tight

As mentioned earlier, wood and sheet-metal screws in most applications rely on friction from the host material to keep them from backing out. Self-tapping and machine screws don't have that advantage, so they have to be kept in place with lock washers or locknuts.

But that's not the end of it. Different materials require different approaches. Most lock washers are only effective where they can be kept under a fair amount of pressure from the screw or nut. That works well for metal-to-metal installations but can be ineffective for joints that include relatively soft materials like plastics and fiberglass, which tend to either creep out of the way or crush in response to excess pressure.

The solution is the use of elastic stop nuts which lock to the screw instead of the material being held. Their only drawback is a tendency to lose their grip after being removed and installed too many times. Other than that, they're nearly infallible.

Loosening

Many things conspire to make threaded fasteners difficult to remove after they've been in place for a while. Boat owners tend to take rust and corrosion for granted, but dirt, dust and other contaminants can work their way under washers and into threads to contribute to the problem, too. A bolt that installed with a power tool at the factory can humble the strongest among us.

Heating the fastener often helps to loosen it, and the application of a lubricant such as WD-40 or Liquid Wrench can make life easier, too. It's also helpful to have tools of the right size and condition. A Phillips screwdriver of the wrong size or one with worn flutes is a losing proposition and will do more damage than good. The same can be said of a standard flat-blade screwdriver.

My favorite cure for recalcitrant bolts and nuts is an impact driver, which looks like a large metal screwdriver handle. One end is equipped with a 3/8" square male drive that will accept standard sockets and screwdriver bits. Its internal mechanism can be set to operate clockwise or in reverse so it can be used to tighten or loosen. With the proper bit in place, set the tool on to or in to the fastener. Put some pressure in the appropriate direction, and give the top of the handle a blow with a stout hammer. The combination of shock and intense twisting motion will loosen the culprit almost every time.

No rules will guarantee that working with threaded hardware will always be easy and problem-free, but choosing the correct hardware, having the right tools and using them properly will go a long way toward making maintenance less frustrating and more successful in the long run.

Keeping It All Together

Many modern conveniences are mounted to fiberglass boats with easy-to-install self-tapping screws threaded into a fiberglass panel. In most cases that works well, but when the screw is overtightened, overloaded or just removed and replaced once too often, you're confronted with a stripped-out hole that will no longer hold the screw or support the accessory.

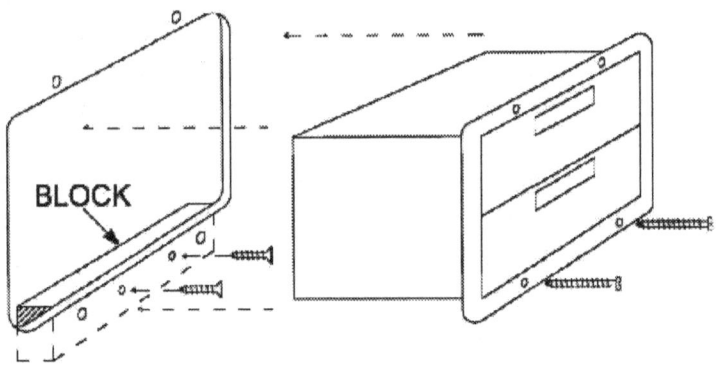

Figure 33-5
Using backing blocks to replace stripped threads.

There are several ways to cure the problem. If you have access to the back of the panel, self-tapping screws can be replaced by machine screws and nuts, using large washers behind the panel to distribute the load. If that's not practical, the problem can be solved by installing a wooden backing block behind the panel and replacing the screws with longer ones that go through the fiberglass and are held by the block. The blocks can be secured to the back of the panel with marine adhesive and small flat-head screws threaded in from the front, but under the footprint of the accessory's flange so they don't show. (See Figure 5.) The screws will hold the block in place and allow you to re-install the accessory immediately without waiting for the adhesive to cure, but the adhesive is still important to ensure a strong long-term bond. Once the blocks are in place, drill pilot holes for the accessory's screws in the blocks to prevent them from splitting, and install the accessory using the original screws (or longer versions if required).

Another solution is the use of T-nuts, available in several sizes at most hardware stores. These are short metal tubes which are internally threaded and have a flange on one end. (See Figure 6.) The tubular part is meant to fit into the stripped-out hole and the flange prevents it from being pulled through. The flange will usually have two or more barbs designed to dig into a soft host material like wood to keep the nut from turning. T-nuts can used in fiberglass by either drilling additional holes on either side to accept the barbs or by cutting off the barbs (leaving a sharp point to help keep them from turning) and relying on an adhesive to keep the nut in place. If the tubular section is too long, it can be filed down or cut with a hacksaw before installation.

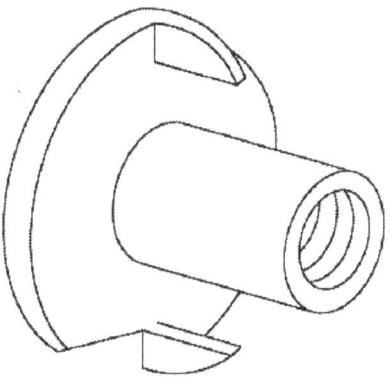

Figure 33-6
A T-nut.

Unfortunately, they're not commonly available in stainless steel, so a liberal coating of silicone sealant should be applied during installation; an extra squirt into the hole before tightening them is a good idea too. The silicone may prevent the nuts from rusting and ensure they'll stick to the back of the panel in case you have to take the screws out again.

By the way, whenever you're threading a screw into fiberglass or wood on a boat, it's a good idea to coat the screw or partially fill the hole with silicone sealant. It lubricates the screw's entry, seals the wood or fiberglass against moisture and then cures to a rubber-like consistency to help lock the screw in place, but not so tightly that you can't get it back out when you need to.

Chapter Thirty-Four
Drilling and Tapping

Precision drilling (creating the right size hole) and tapping (forming internal threads to accommodate a screw or bolt) are normally the bailiwick of machinists and tool-makers, but anyone who takes a hands-on approach to maintaining or improving a boat will confront the need to do one or both eventually.

Drilling

Drilling the right size hole is important in three operations: creating a clearance hole for a screw or other hardware to pass through freely, providing a pilot hole to ease the entry of a self-tapping or sheet-metal screw, and making a hole which will be tapped with internal threads to accept a machine screw.

The ability to drill the right size hole is made possible by the availability of 135 standard sizes of drills under 1/2" in diameter, not including metric sizes. (See Appendix B.) There are larger ones, but they are best left to the pros. While a non-professional may only need a small number of drills, it's important to get the right ones. Three sets of drills make up the 135. There are 29 fractional drills, ranging in size from 1/16" to 1/2" in 1/64" increments, 80 numbered drills (#1 through #80) from .013" to .228", and 26 letter drills (A to Z) from .234" to .413". It's not necessary to buy complete sets.

Good hardware or industrial supply stores sell at least the more popular sizes individually.

The basic rules are fairly straightforward:

Do not attempt to drill large holes in thin material. In general, limit the size to about 1.5 times the material's thickness. If you need a larger hole in thin material, form it with a tapered reamer.

Hold the electric drill firmly and perpendicular to the work.

Match the drill speed to the hole size; the larger the drill, the slower it should turn.

Lubricate the drill tip with cutting oil or light machine oil when drilling into thick metal, but use a dry bit in absorbent materials such as wood and fiberglass.

For large holes, start with a small one and work your way up in stages with increasingly larger drill bits, and always wear eye protection.

Tapping

Tapping requires a more delicate touch and more care than drilling holes but is still within the capabilities of a careful craftsman. Taps are short, externally threaded rods with flutes machined along the length of the threaded portion. The flutes interrupt the threads, leaving extremely sharp cutting edges which form internal threads in the material as the tap is twisted down into a hole. The flutes also serve as an expansion chamber to collect and carry away the chips created during the process. The top of the tap is usually square to fit into and be driven by a tapping wrench.

Taps for a specific thread are often sold in sets of three: a taper tap which makes starting easier, a plug tap which will form threads more completely in a deep hole, and a bottoming tap which will form threads nearly all the way to the bottom of a blind hole. Common practice is to use the first two (or even all three) types in succession for a good job without tool breakage.

Taps should never be used in metal without the application of a cutting oil or lubricant. In order to stand up to the rigors of their task, they are hardened to extreme levels during their manufacture, leaving them quite brittle and subject to shattering under excess stress. It is imperative to wear not just glasses but safety goggles to provide adequate eye protection when using them.

The basic rules for using taps are:

Start with the exactly correct size pilot hole (See chart below).

Start with a taper tap to ensure a straight beginning and ease of entry.

If the effort required to turn the tap increases, back off a turn or so, then proceed.

Don't allow metal chips to build up in the flutes. Back the tap all the way out, clean it and begin again if necessary.

TAP DRILL AND CLEARANCE DRILL SIZES FOR COMMON SCREWS
All sizes and dimensions in inches

SCREW SIZE	TAP DRILL SIZE	CLEARANCE DRILL SIZE
4-40	#43	1/8
6-32	#36	5/32
8-32	#29	11/64
10-24	#25	13/64
10-32	#21	13/64
12-24	#16	7/32
1/4-20	#7	17/64
5/16-18	F	21/64
3/8-16	5/16	25/64

Modern Boatworks -- *By David S. Yetman*

Figure 34-1

Appendix A
Publication Credits

Parts or all of Chapters 20, 22, 25, 26, 28, 32 and 33 were originally published in various issues of *Motorboating & Sailing* magazine and are reprinted here with its courtesy. Parts or all of Chapters 30 and 31, originally appeared in various issues of *Power & Motoryacht* magazine and are reprinted here with its courtesy.

Portions of Chapter 6 were originally published as part of an article co-authored by Richard Thiel in the June, 1999 issue of *Power & Motoryacht*. No part of Mr. Thiel's contribution is included here.

Parts of Chapters 17 and 20 were originally published in various issues of *Sail* magazine, reprinted here with its courtesy.

Parts or all of Chapters 8, 14, 15 and 19 were originally published in *Soundings*.

Parts or all of Chapters 2, 9, 10, 11, 12, 16, 18, 21, 27 and 29 originally were published in various issues of *Trailer Boats magazine*.

Part or all of Chapters 23 and 24 originally appeared in various issues of *Yachting* magazine.

Modern Boatworks -- *By David S. Yetman*

Appendix B
Numbered Drill Sizes

SIZE	DIA.	SIZE	DIA.	SIZE	DIA.	SIZE	DIA.	SIZE	DIA.
1	0.288	17	0.173	33	0.113	49	0.073	65	0.035
2	0.221	18	0.169	34	0.111	50	0.070	66	0.033
3	0.213	19	0.166	35	0.110	51	0.067	67	0.032
4	0.209	20	0.161	36	0.106	52	0.063	68	0.031
5	0.205	21	0.159	37	0.104	53	0.059	69	0.029
6	0.204	22	0.157	38	0.101	54	0.055	70	0.028
7	0.201	23	0.154	39	0.099	55	0.052	71	0.026
8	0.199	24	0.152	40	0.098	56	0.046	72	0.025
9	0.196	25	0.149	41	0.096	57	0.043	73	0.024
10	0.193	26	0.147	42	0.093	58	0.042	74	0.022
11	0.191	27	0.144	43	0.089	59	0.041	75	0.021
12	0.189	28	0.140	44	0.086	60	0.040	76	0.020
13	0.185	29	0.136	45	0.082	61	0.039	77	0.018
14	0.182	30	0.128	46	0.081	62	0.038	78	0.016
15	0.180	31	0.120	47	0.078	63	0.037	79	0.014
16	0.177	32	0.116	48	0.076	64	0.036	80	0.013

Dimensions are in inches.

Lettered Drill Sizes

SIZE	DIA.	SIZE	DIA.	SIZE	DIA.	SIZE	DIA.	SIZE	DIA.
A	0.234	G	0.261	L	0.290	Q	0.332	V	0.377
B	0.238	H	0.266	M	0.295	R	0.339	W	0.386
C	0.242	I	0.272	N	0.302	S	0.348	X	0.397
D	0.246	J	0.277	O	0.316	T	0.358	Y	0.404
E	0.250	K	0.281	P	0.323	U	0.368	Z	0.413
F	0.257								

Dimensions are in inches.

Modern Boatworks -- *By David S. Yetman*

Appendix C
Decimal - Metric - Fraction Conversion

FRAC INCH	DEC INCH	mm	FRAC INCH	DEC INCH	mm	FRAC INCH	DEC INCH	mm
1/64	0.016	0.397	23/64	0.359	9.130	45/64	0.703	17.860
1/32	0.031	0.794	**3/8**	**0.375**	**9.530**	23/32	0.719	18.260
3/64	0.047	1.190	25/64	0.391	9.920	47/64	0.734	18.650
1/16	**0.062**	**1.590**	13/32	0.406	10.320	**3/4**	**0.750**	**19.050**
5/64	0.071	1.980	27/64	0.422	10.720	49/64	0.766	19.450
3/32	0.094	2.380	**7/16**	**0.437**	**11.110**	25/32	0.781	19.840
7/64	0.109	2.780	29/64	0.453	11.510	51/64	0.897	20.240
1/8	**0.125**	**3.170**	15/32	0.469	11.910	**13/16**	**0.813**	**20.640**
9/64	0.141	3.570	31/64	0.484	12.300	53/64	0.828	21.030
5/32	0.156	3.970	**1/2**	**0.500**	**12.700**	27/32	0.844	21.430
11/64	0.172	4.370	33/64	0.516	13.100	55/64	0.859	21.820
3/16	**0.188**	**4.760**	17/32	0.531	13.490	**7/8**	**0.875**	**22.230**
13/6	0.203	5.160	35/64	0.547	13.89	57/64	0.891	22.6
7/32	0.219	5.560	**9/16**	**0.562**	**14.29**	29/32	0.906	23.0
15/6	0.234	5.950	37/64	0.578	14.68	59/64	0.922	23.4
1/4	**0.250**	**6.350**	19/32	0.594	15.08	**15/16**	**0.938**	**23.8**
17/6	0.266	6.750	39/64	0.609	15.48	61/64	0.953	24.2
9/32	0.281	7.140	**5/8**	**0.625**	**15.87**	31/32	0.969	24.6
19/6	0.297	7.540	41/64	0.641	16.27	63/64	0.984	25.0
5/16	**0.312**	**7.940**	21/32	0.656	16.67	**1**	**1.000**	**25.4**
21/6	0.328	8.330	43/64	0.672	17.07			
11/3	0.344	8.730	**11/16**	**0.688**	**17.46**			

Decimal and metric equivalents have been rounded up to next hundredth or thousandth.

Modern Boatworks -- By David S. Yetman

Books Published by Bristol Fashion Publications

www.wescottcovepublishing.com

Boat Repair Made Easy — Haul Out
Written By John P. Kaufman

Boat Repair Made Easy — Finishes
Written By John P. Kaufman

Boat Repair Made Easy — Systems
Written By John P. Kaufman

Boat Repair Made Easy — Engines
Written By John P. Kaufman

Standard Ship's Log
Designed By John P. Kaufman

Large Ship's Log
Designed By John P. Kaufman

Custom Ship's Log
Designed By John P. Kaufman

Designing Power & Sail
Written By Arthur Edmunds

Fiberglass Boat Survey
Written By Arthur Edmunds

Building a Fiberglass Boat
Written By Arthur Edmunds

Buying a Great Boat
Written By Arthur Edmunds

**Outfitting & Organizing Your Boat
For A Day, A Week or A Lifetime**
Written By Michael L. Frankel

Boater's Book of Nautical Terms
Written By David S. Yetman

Modern Boatworks
Written By David S. Yetman

Practical Seamanship
Written By David S. Yetman

Practical Seamanship
Written By David S. Yetman

Captain Jack's Basic Navigation
Written By Jack I. Davis

Captain Jack's Celestial Navigation
Written By Jack I. Davis

Captain Jack's Complete Navigation
Written By Jack I. Davis

Southwinds Gourmet
Written By Susan Garrett Mason

The Cruising Sailor
Written By Tom Dove

Building a Fiberglass Boat
Written By Arthur Edmunds

Daddy & I Go Boating
Written By Ken Kreisler

My Grandpa Is a Tugboat Captain
Written By Ken Kreisler

Billy the Oysterman
Written By Ken Kreisler

Modern Boatworks -- By David S. Yetman

Creating Comfort Afloat
Written By Janet Groene

Living Aboard
Written By Janet Groene

Simple Boat Projects
Written By Donald Boone

Racing the Ice to Cape Horn
Written By Frank Guernsey & Cy Zoerner

Boater's Checklist
Written By Clay Kelley

**Florida Through the Islands
What Boaters Need To Know**
Written By Captain Clay Kelley & Marybeth

Marine Weather Forecasting
Written By J. Frank Brumbaugh

Basic Boat Maintenance
Written By J. Frank Brumbaugh

Complete Guide to Gasoline Marine Engines
Written By John Fleming

Complete Guide to Outboard Engines
Written By John Fleming

Complete Guide to Diesel Marine Engines
Written By John Fleming

Trouble Shooting Gasoline Marine Engines
Written By John Fleming

Trailer Boats
Written By Alex Zidock

Skipper's Handbook
Written By Robert S. Grossman

Modern Boatworks -- By David S. Yetman

Wake Up & Water Ski
Written By Kimberly P. Robinson

White Squall - The Last Voyage of Albatross
Written By Richard E. Langford

**Cruising South
What to Expect Along the ICW**
Written By Joan Healy

Electronics Aboard
Written By Stephen Fishman

**A Whale at the Port Quarter
A Treasure Chest of Sea Stories**
Written By Charles Gnaegy

REVIEWS

Lakeland Boating
JUST DO IT YOURSELF

Aimed at the hands-on boat owner, Modern Boatworks covers mechanical, electrical, communications and maintenance info. Even if you're not quite ready to tackle an overhaul of your boat's electrical system, author David S. Yetman gives the lowdown on other improvement projects, along with the scoop on which tools to use. But the publishers say this isn't just another DIY text. There are also several chapters on the fine art of maintenance and some tips for taking the drudgery out of less pleasant tasks.

Modern Boatworks -- By David S. Yetman

Trailer Boats
GOTTA HAVE IT

Trailer Boats Columnist Tells All In Practical New Book

New from Bristol Fashion Publications is Modern Boatworks, by Trailer Boats' "Boat Improvement" columnist David S. Yetman. The 244-page, illustrated book covers a wide range of topics of interest to hands-on boaters, and provides information on mechanical, electrical, communications and maintenance on board. Many of the chapters are designed to help the reader understand, use and fix some of the newer technologies. Other chapters walk the reader through improvement projects and the fine art of maintenance. This practical book is aimed at all experience levels.

Offshore - Holly Parker and Lisa Fabian

If you're a hands-on boat owner, this practical guide is for you. Improvement projects, the correct tools to use and helpful hints inform boaters on how they can operate, maintain and improve their boats. For those who are technologically inclined and wish to gain a better understanding of their boat, Modern Boatworks offers detailed advice.

Boating World

Sticking to the latest technologies most average boaters may be interested in, Yetman's essays are written in accessible layman's terms and include topics such as "Propulsion Choices," Surviving A Mechanical Emergency," and even how to apply vinyl letters to name your boat. Illustrated with simple, straightforward photos, the book is an easy-to-use reference for folks who enjoy maintaining and improving their own boats.

Soundings
Practical advice for modern boaters

Bristol Fashion Publications is publishing two books by David S. Yetman this year.

"Modern Boatworks," (January 2001 $24.95) tries to cover all aspects of the modern boat. It tackles the mechanical, electrical, communication and maintenance aspects of boating. Yetman also offers some do-it-yourself projects, such as customizing your instrument panel and resurrecting dinged propellers. The 244-page book is divided into 34 chapters, designed to promote browsing and easy access to the areas of modern boating that interest you most.

Yetman doesn't harbor any illusions about what his second release this year, "Practical Seamanship" (March 2001, S17.95), can manage in 116 pages. "The goal of 'Practical Seamanship' is not to make a bluewater cruiser out of every reader, but to provide the basics to help them handle their boats in a knowledgeable, responsible manner," writes Yetman in a press release.

Yetman breaks those basics down into straightforward chapters like maneuverability, External Influences, Docking, Handling Heavy Seas and The Very Unofficial Rules of the Road. There are plenty of simple, clear illustrations throughout the book to help the reader grasp the points. But as the author points out in the first chapter, only experience can help you truly master boat handling.

In both books, Yetman approaches each topic with a mix of experience, science and explanation that manages to be simple without being simplistic.

Modern Boatworks -- By David S. Yetman

About the Author

Dave Yetman is a lifelong New Englander who's spent most of his adult life within sight of the water and comes by his nautical interests quite naturally. His seafaring ancestors include Labrador fishermen and lighthouse keepers and a Cape Cod grandfather who was an inventor and shipbuilder and noted for his models of historic New England lighthouses.

His own career has been in mechanical design and engineering, first as an entrepreneur and later as an engineering manager for an international technology company. He's been awarded patents for a wide range of devices, from motorcycle frames to biomedical laboratory instruments and enjoys applying his talents to his boats, which usually end up in a highly customized state.

His work has been widely published in the boating press and was recognized with awards in the 1997 and 1999 Boating Writers International writing competition. His articles, photography and technical illustrations have been published in *Boating World, Lakeland Boating, Motorboating, Offshore, Power & Motoryacht, Sail, Soundings, Trailer Boats* and *Yachting* magazines. He has three books to his credit, "The Boaters' Book of Nautical Terms", "Modern Boatworks" and "Practical Seamanship".

Dave and his wife, Pat enjoy cruising the New England coast on *CURMUDGEON*, their Albin Tournament Express convertible.

Modern Boatworks -- *By David S. Yetman*

www.ingramcontent.com/pod-product-compliance
Lightning Source LLC
Chambersburg PA
CBHW022110150426
43195CB00008B/341